ASTRA ZERO

Dark Vintage

COLLECTION

VOL.3

A DARK AND SEXY COLLECTION OF ART
INSPIRED BY MIXING AND REVAMPING OLD HISTORICAL ARTWORK
WITH A MORE EROTIC, MUSCULAR MALE BODY DRIVEN AND
SOMETIMES HORROR THEMED LENS

BY GAY ALTERNATIVE CANADIAN ARTIST: ASTRA ZERO

THIS BOOK IS MADE FOR ADULTS ONLY 18+

astrazero.com 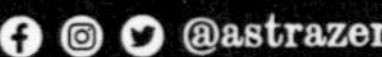 @astrazero

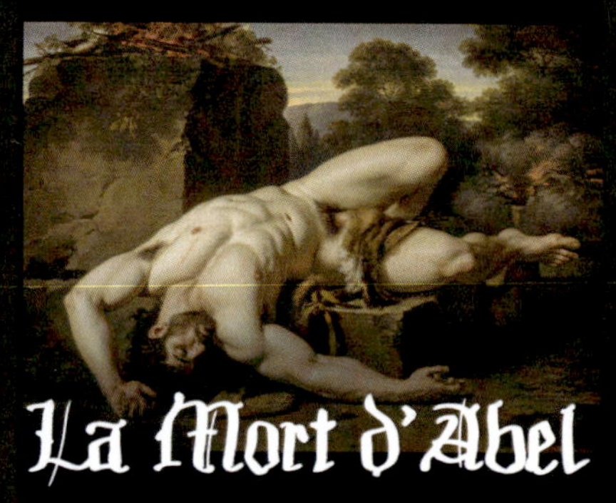

ASTRA ZERO REVAMP OF,
LA MORT D'ABEL,
BY FRANCOIS-XAVIER FABRE, 1790

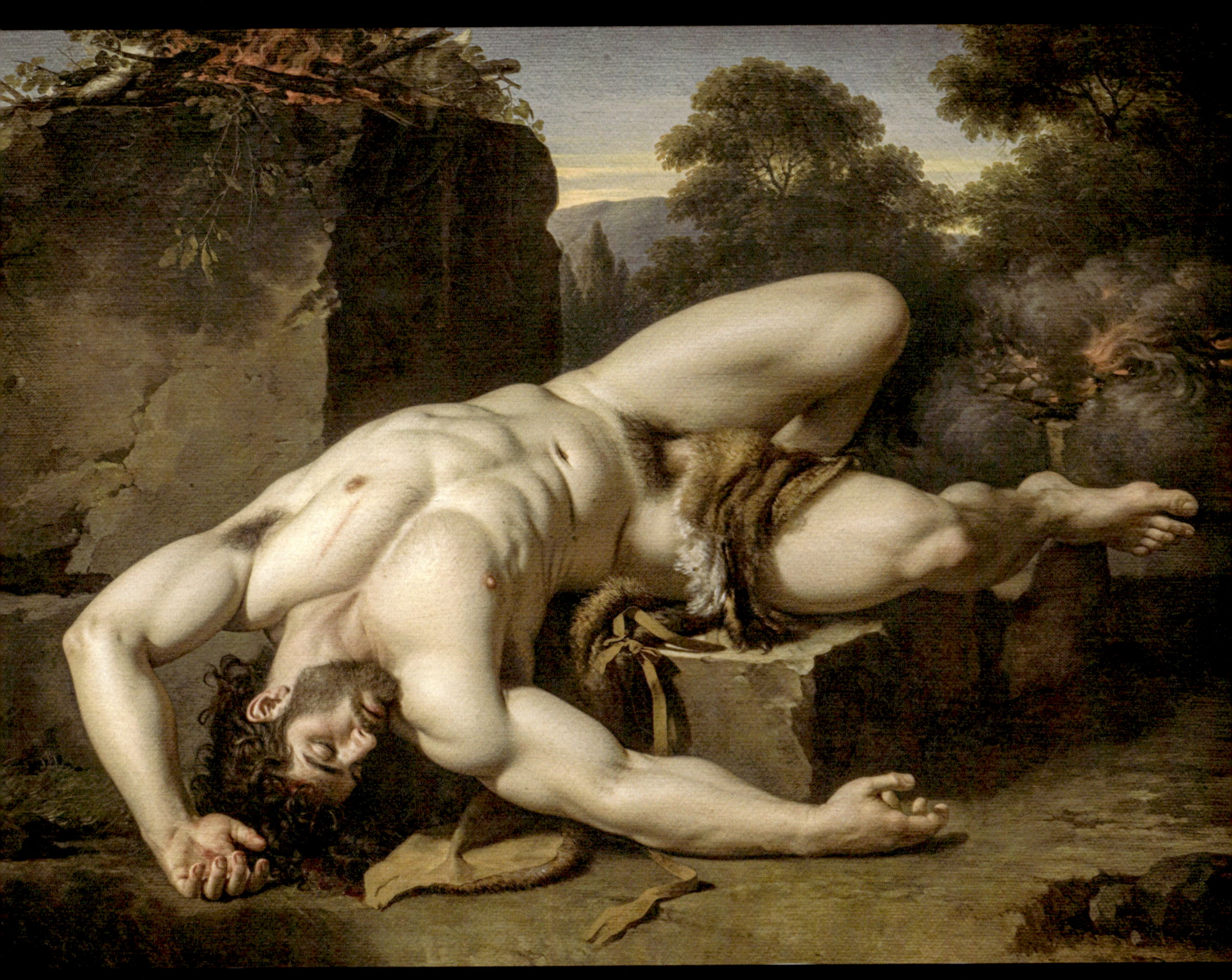

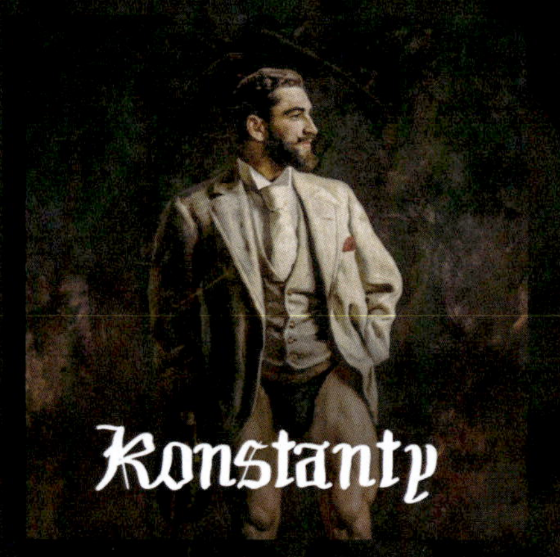

Konstanty

ASTRA ZERO REVAMP OF,
PORTRAIT, BY
KONSTANTY GORSKI, 1896

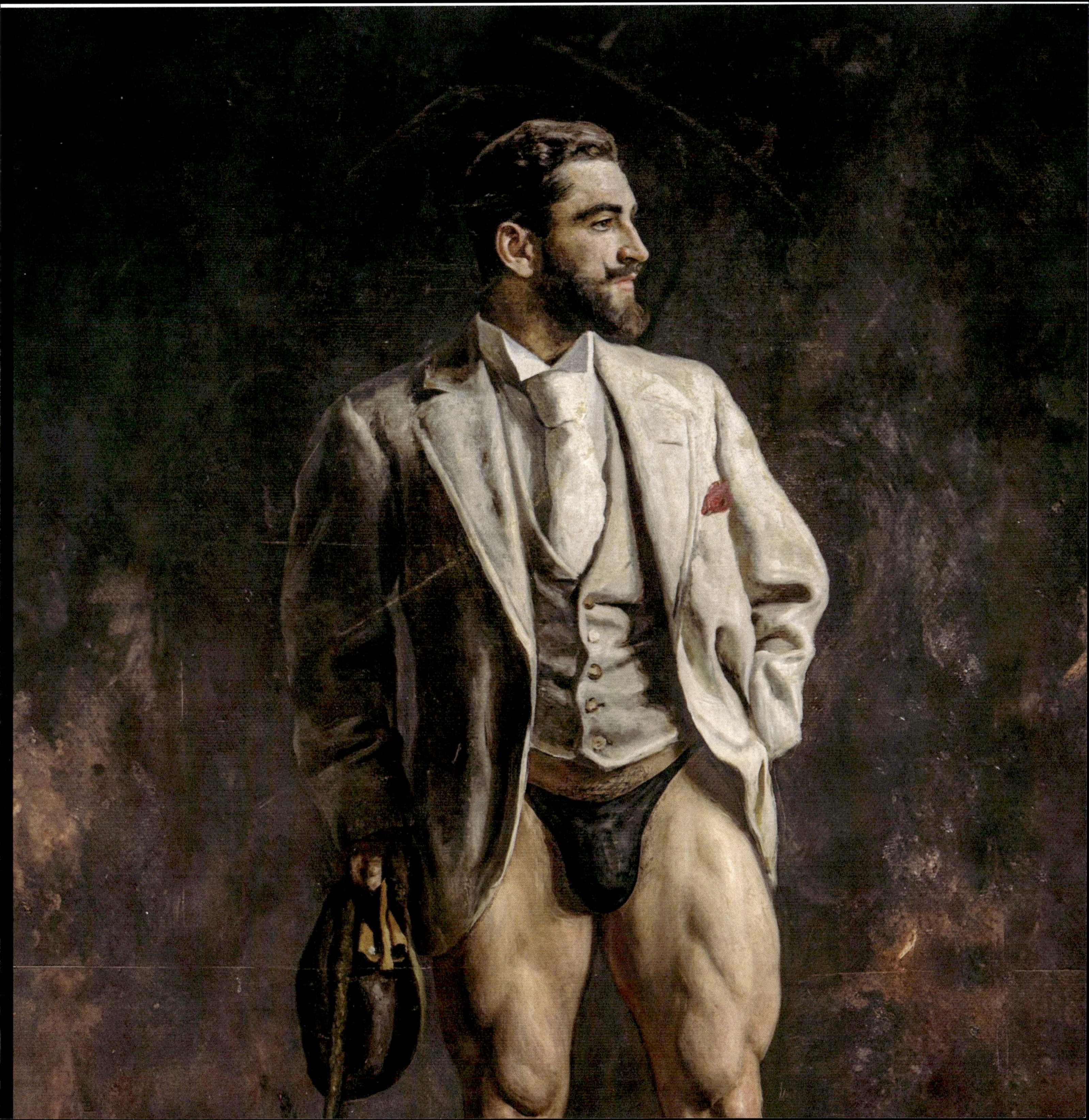

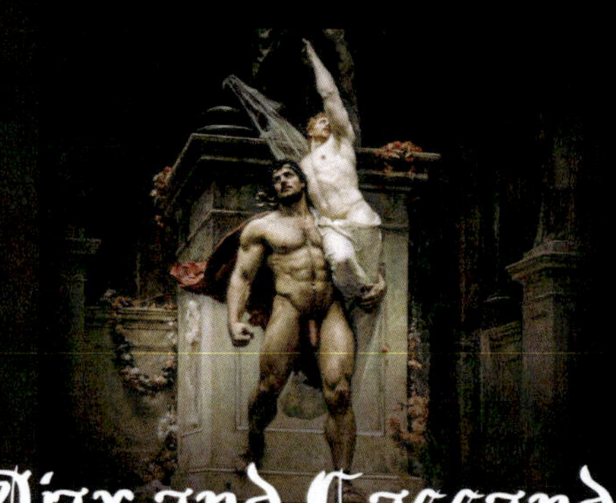

Ajax and Cassander

ASTRA ZERO REVAMP OF,
AJAX AND CASSANDRA, BY
SOLOMON JOSEPH SOLOMON, 1886

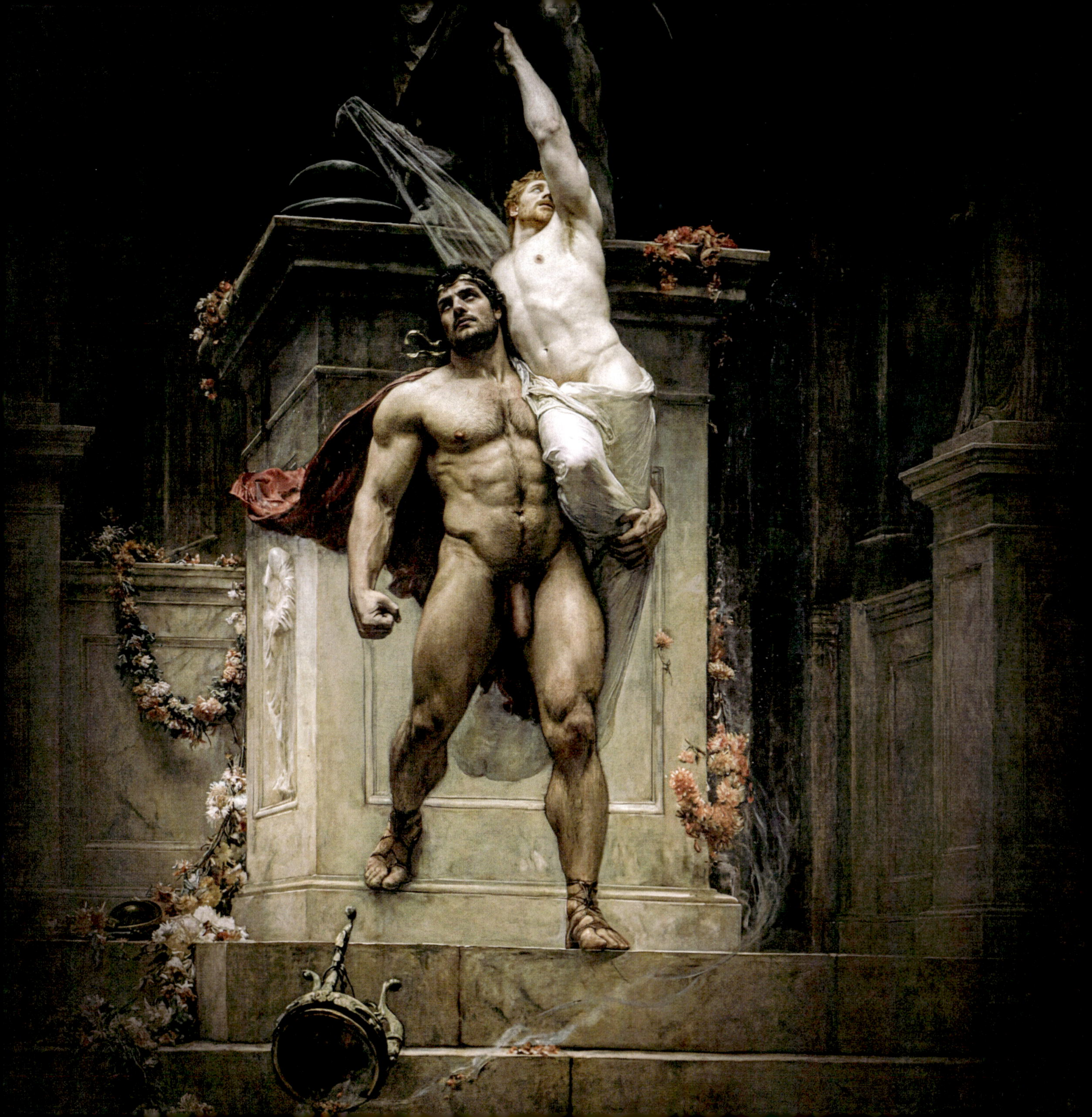

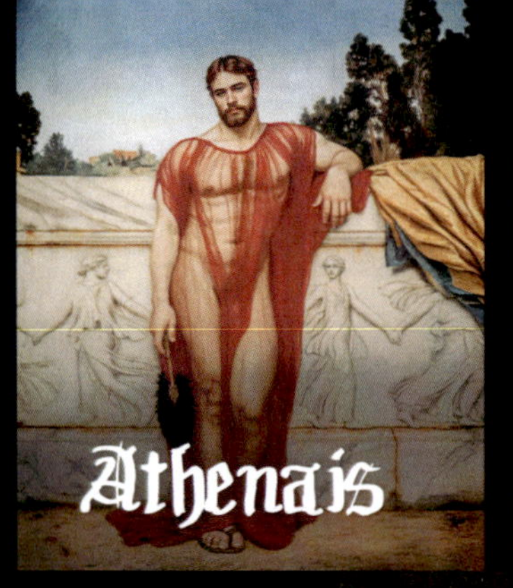

ASTRA ZERO REVAMP OF,
ATHENAIS, BY
OHN WILLIAM GODWARD, 1908

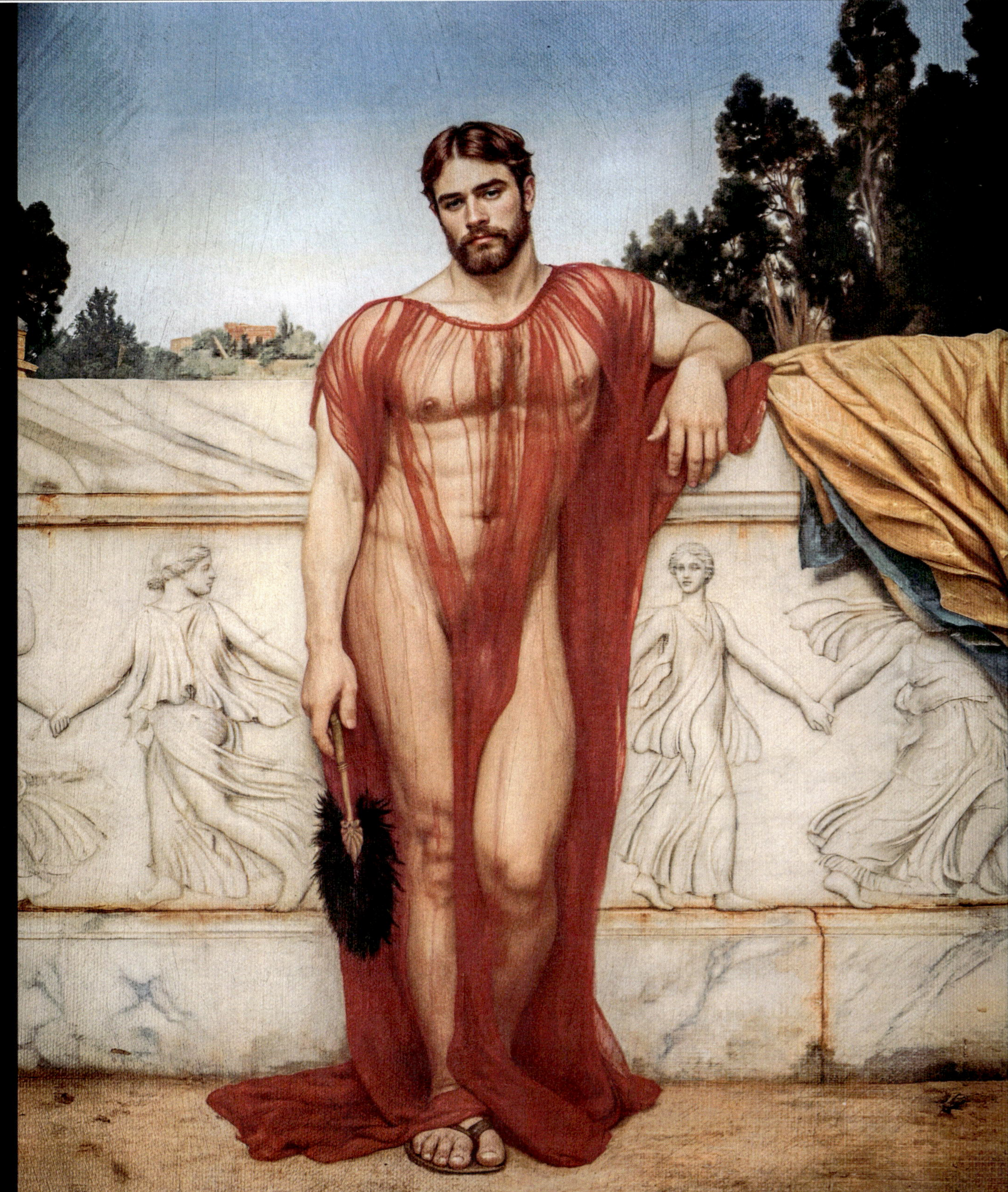

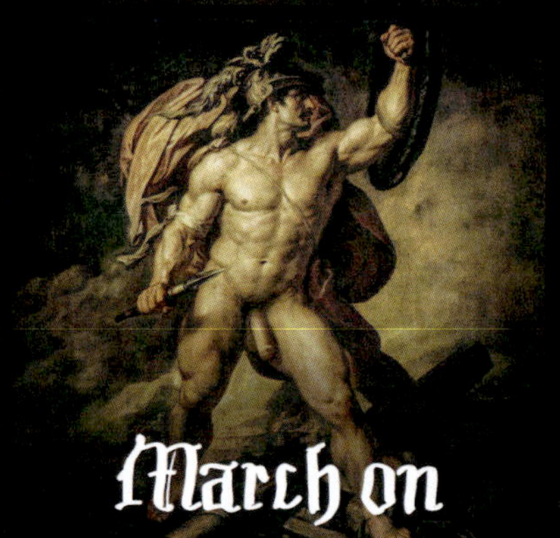

March on

ASTRA ZERO REVAMP OF,
MARS OP HET SLAGVELD, BY
BARTHOLOMEUS SPRANGER, 1580

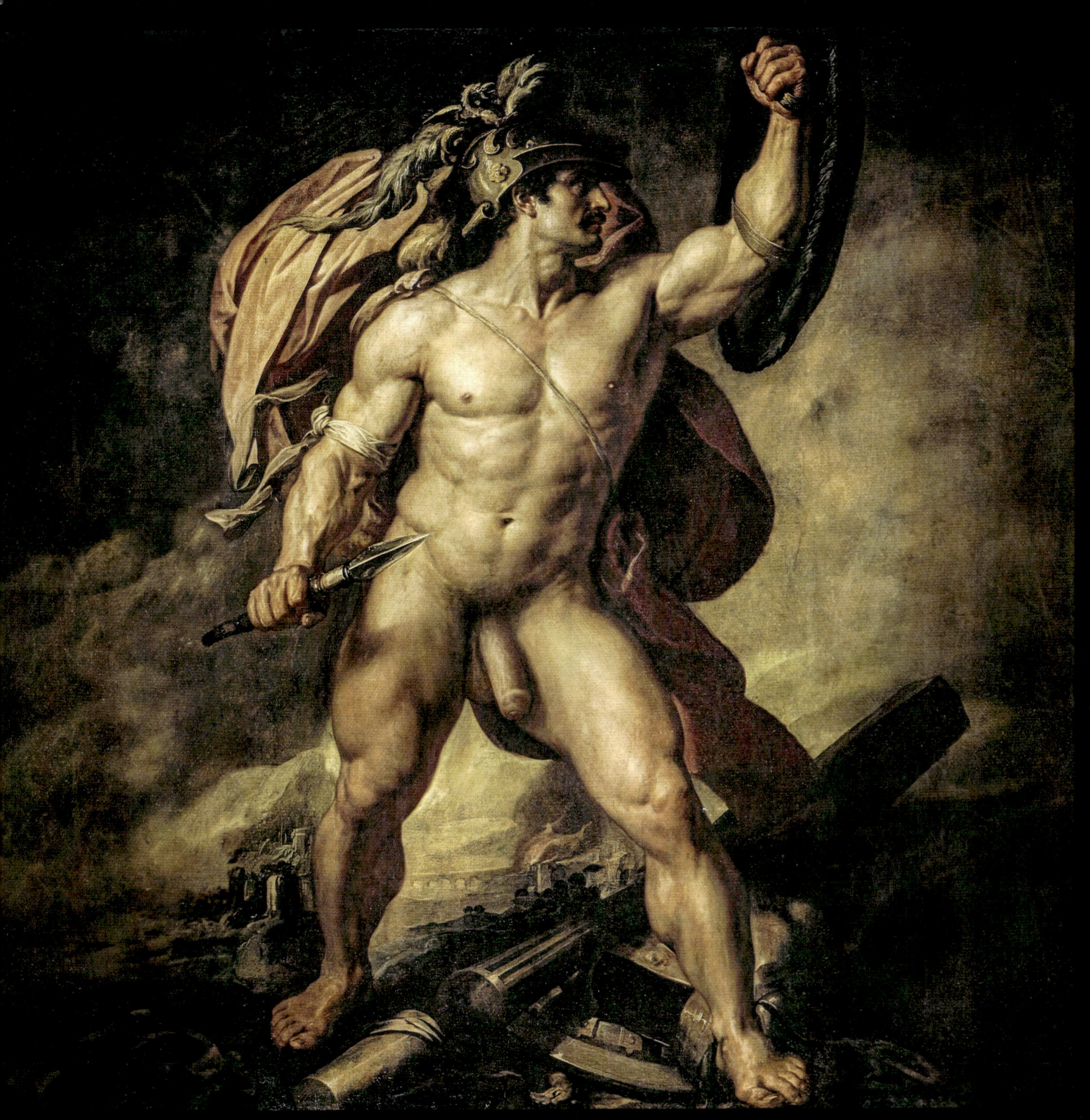

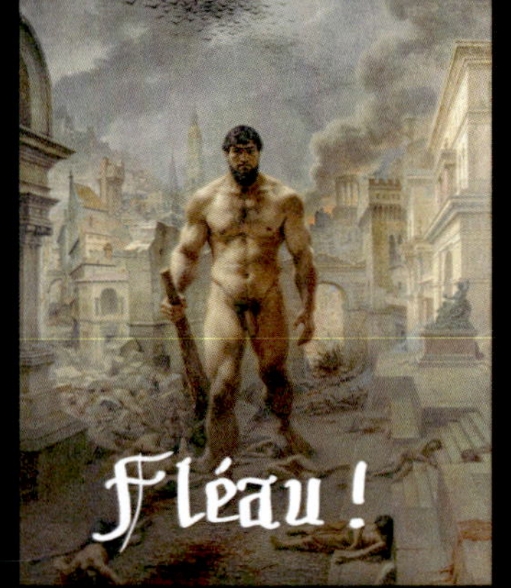

ASTRA ZERO REVAMP OF,
FLEAU !, BY
HENRI-CAMILLE DANGER, 1901

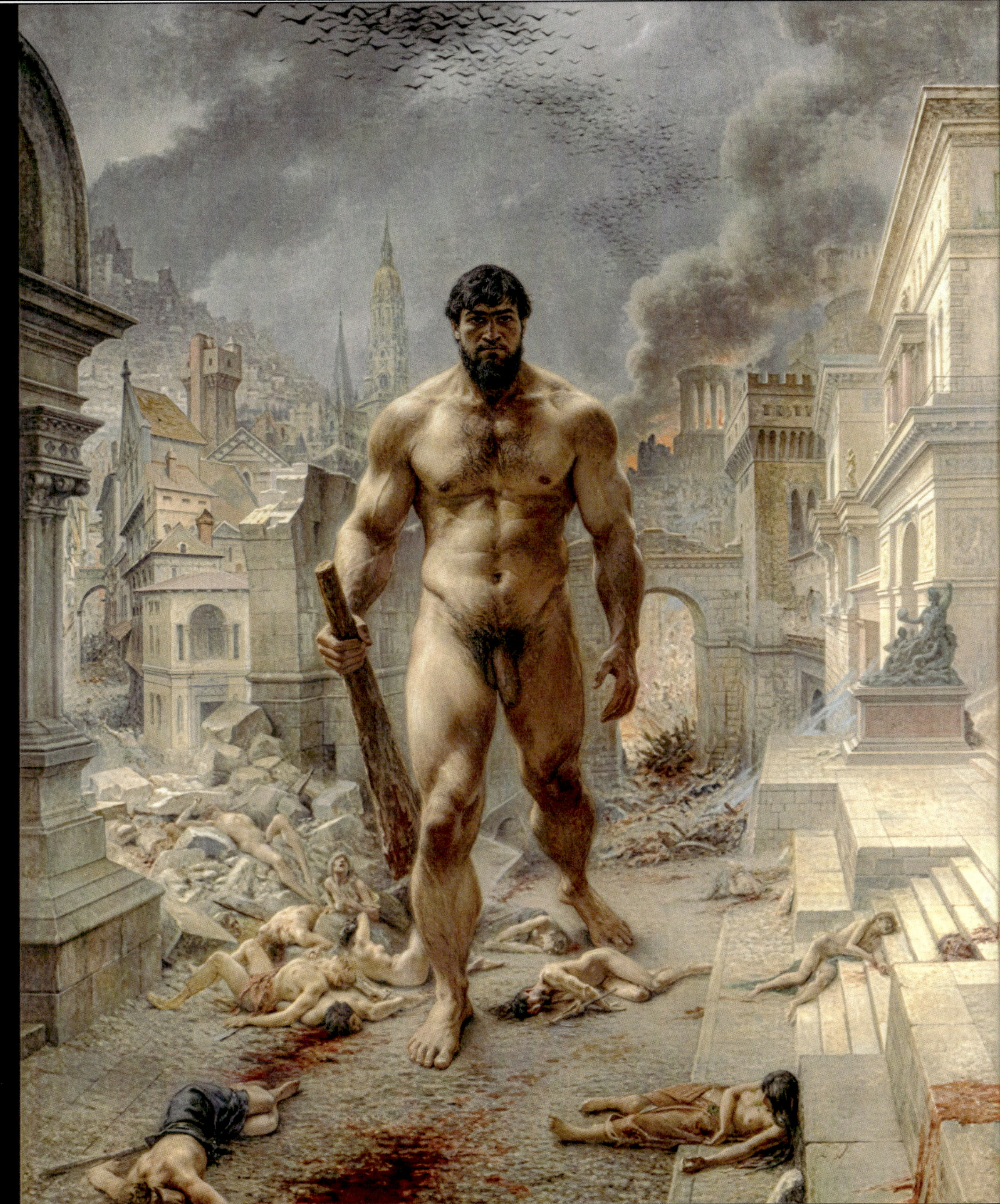

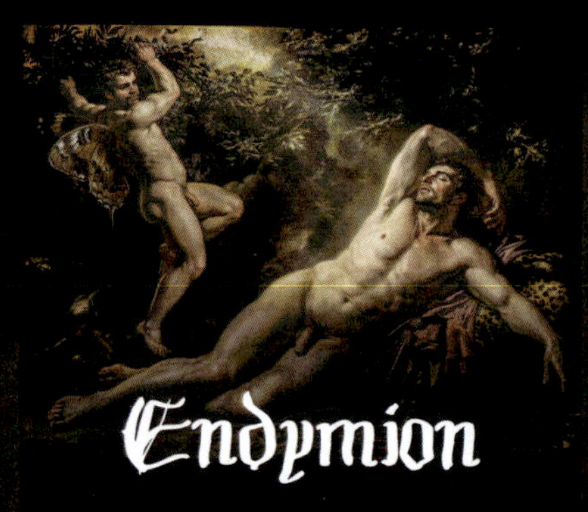

ASTRA ZERO REVAMP
OF ENDYMION
BY ANNE-LOUIS GIRODET
DE ROUSSY-TRIOSON, 1791

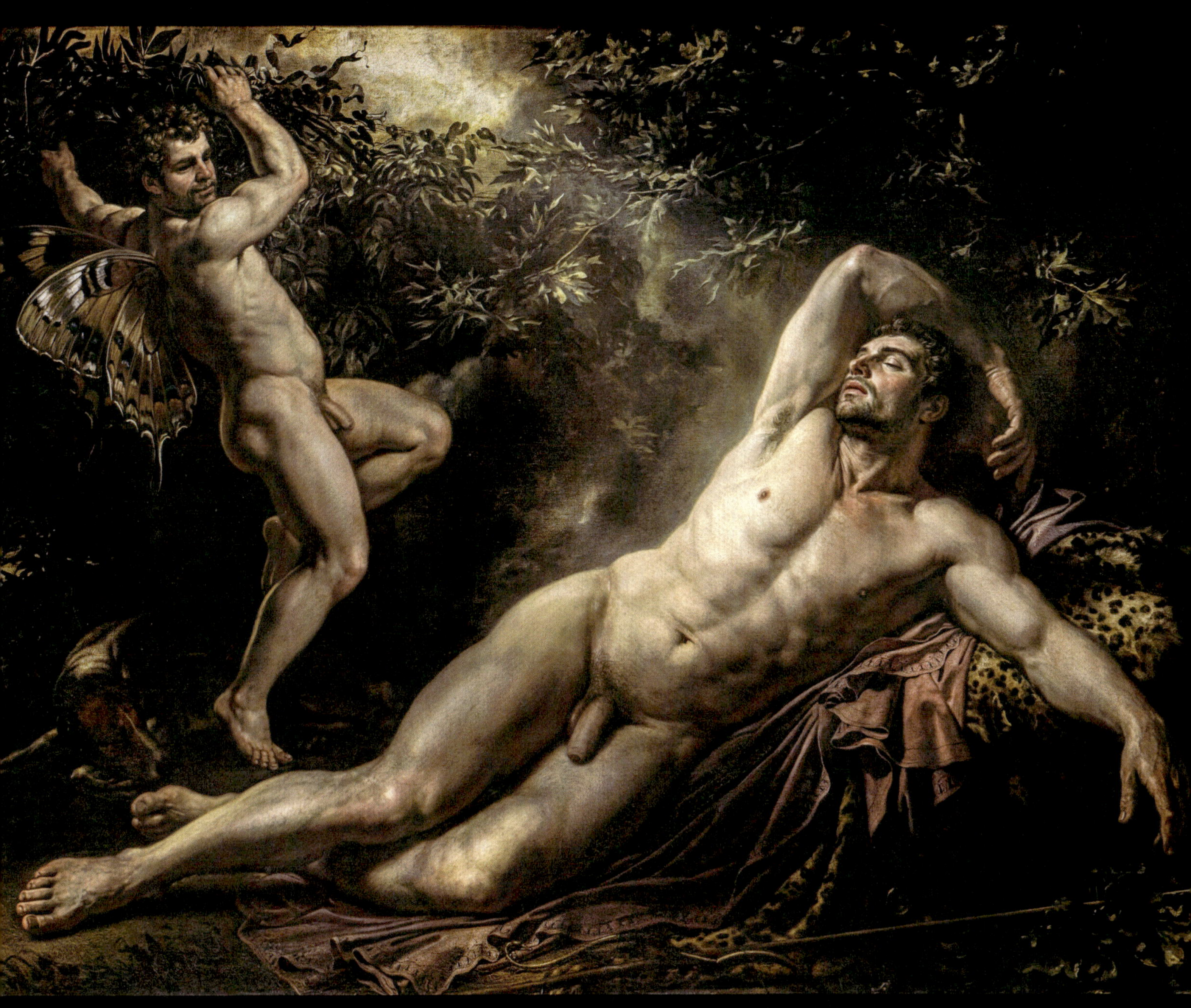

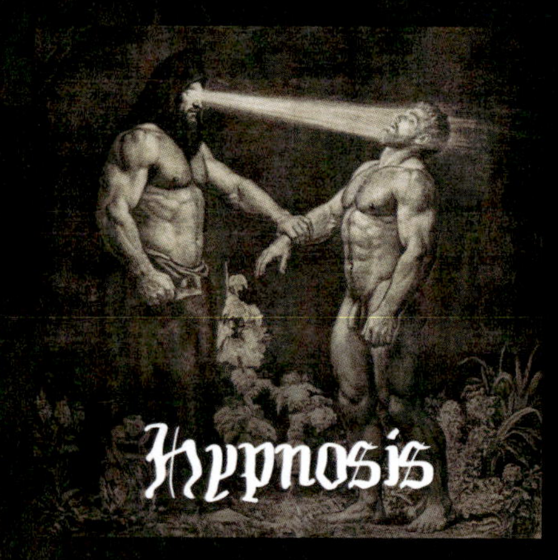

ASTRA ZERO REVAMP OF,
HYPNOSIS, BY
SASCHA SCHNEIDER, 1904

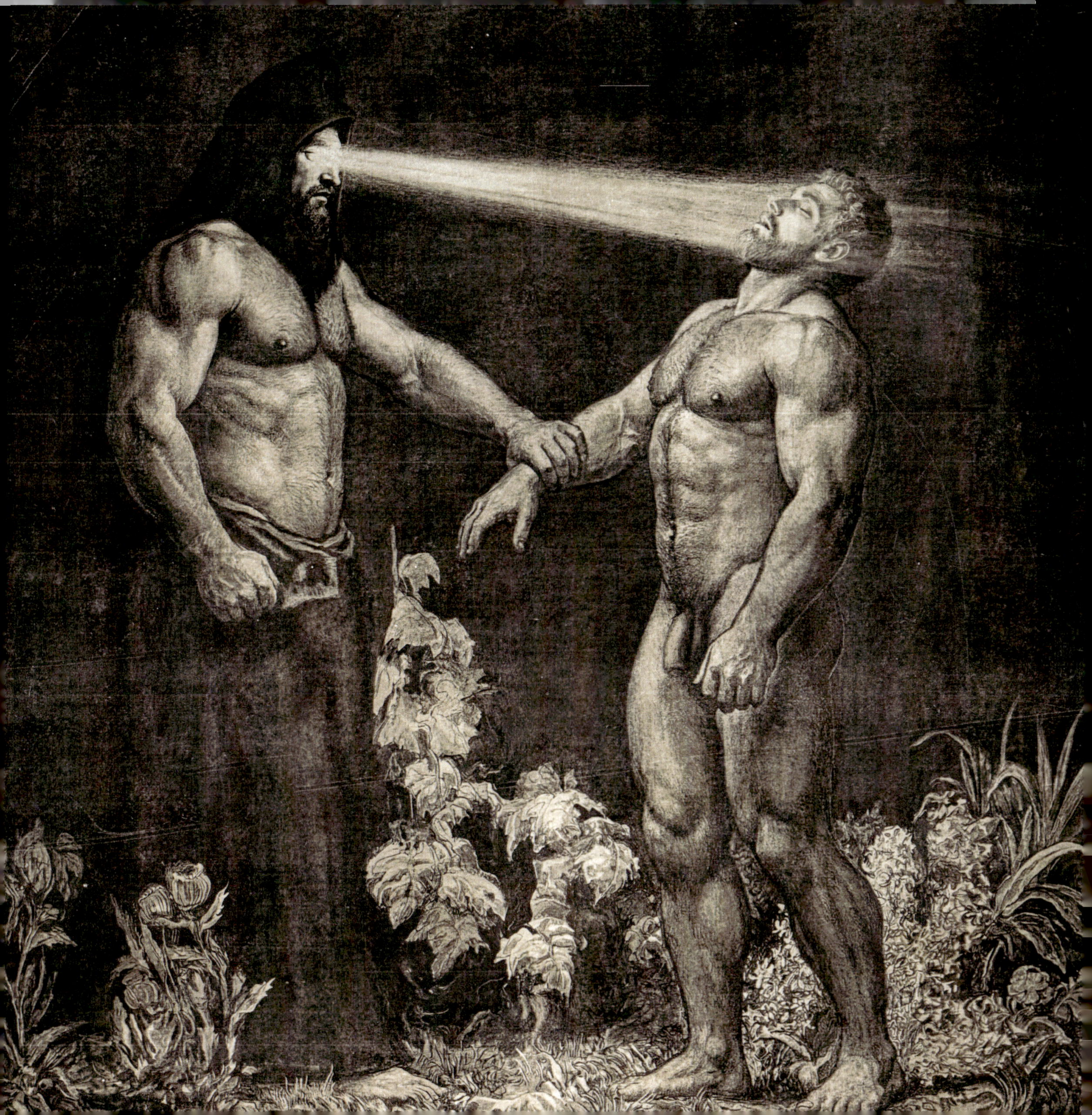

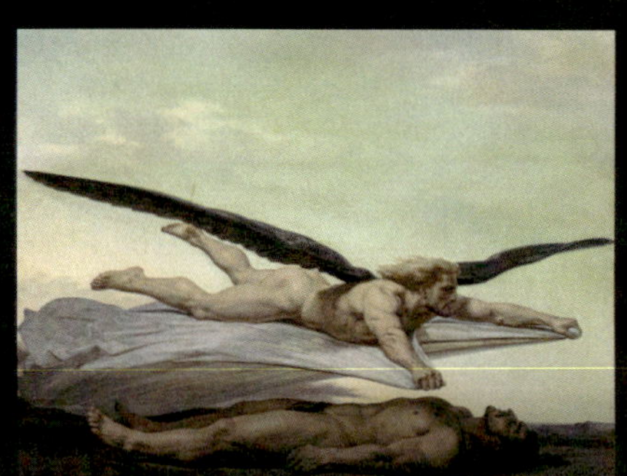

ASTRA ZERO REVAMP OF,
EGALITE DEVANT LA MORT, BY
WILLIAM BOUGUEREAU, 1848

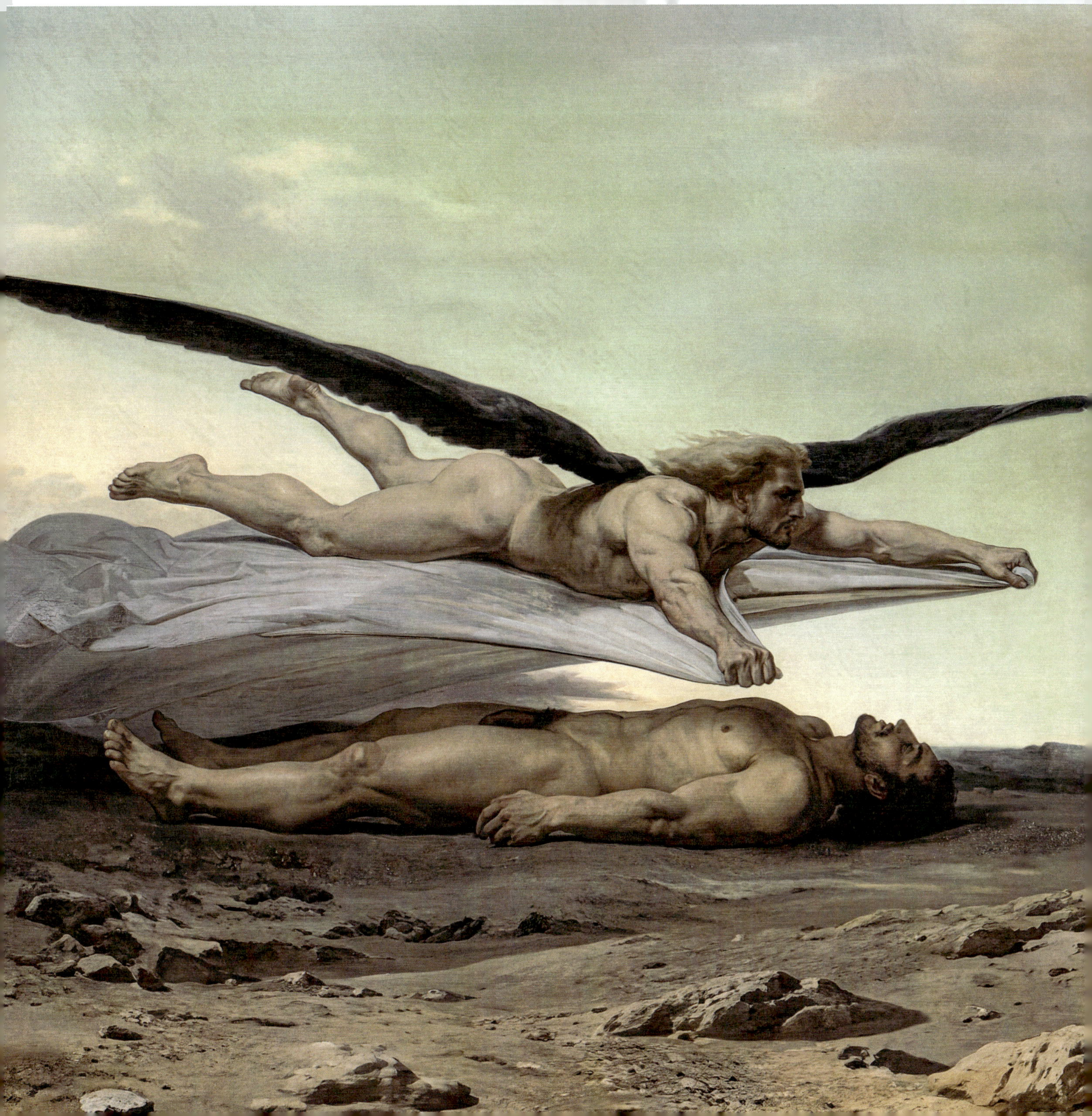

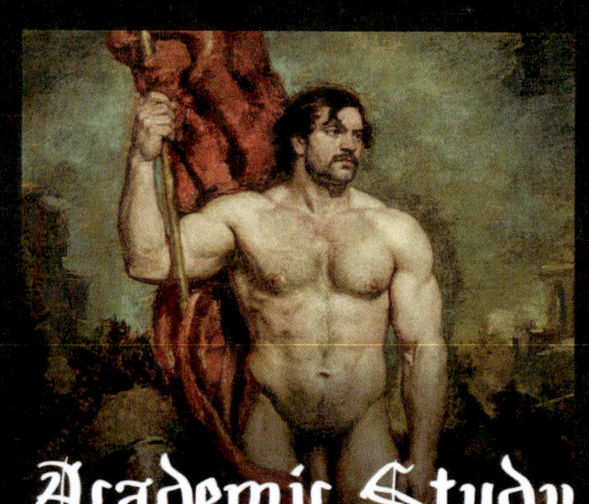

Academic Study

ASTRA ZERO REVAMP OF,
ACADEMIC STUDY, BY
WILLIAM ETTY, 1843

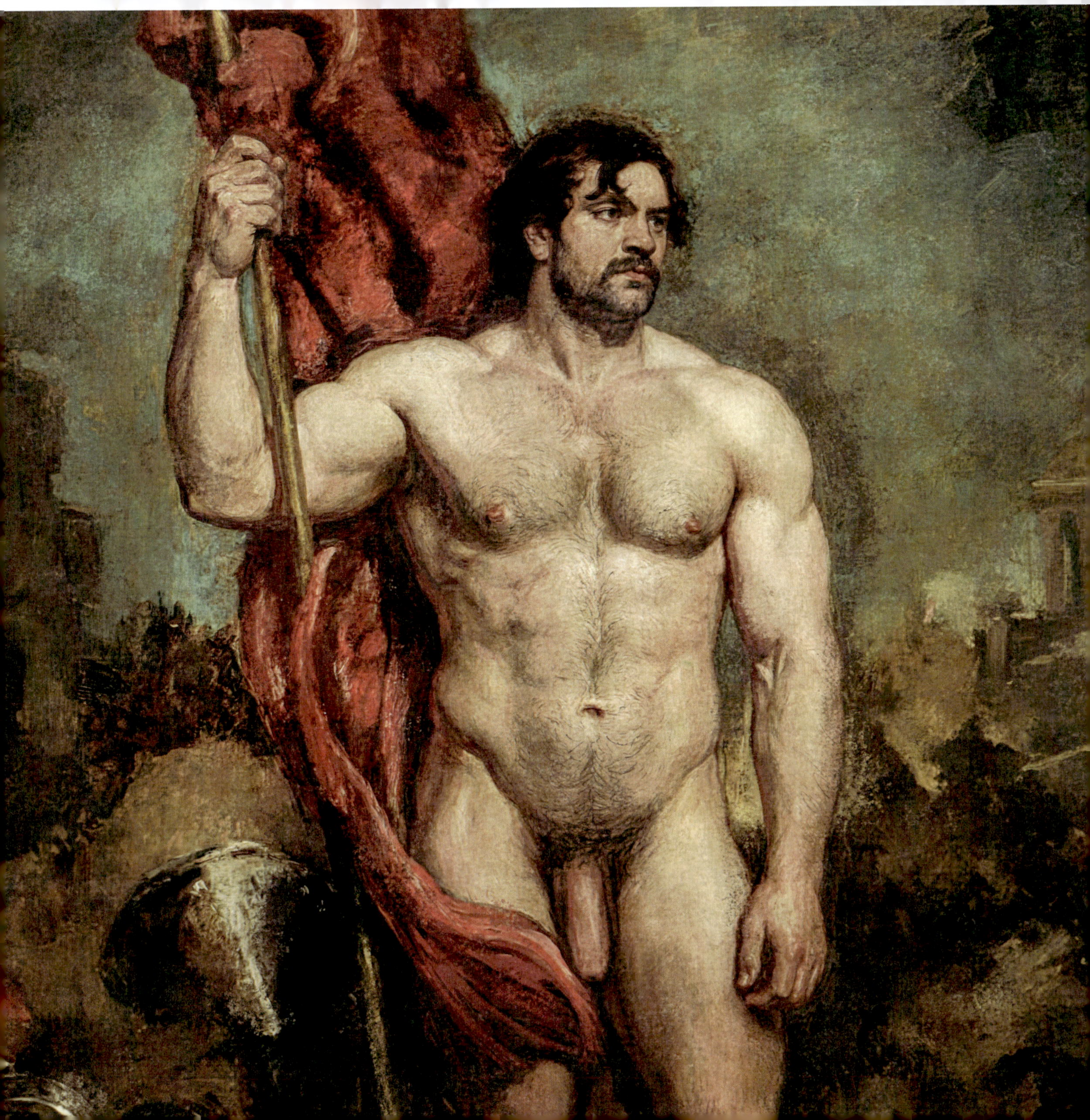

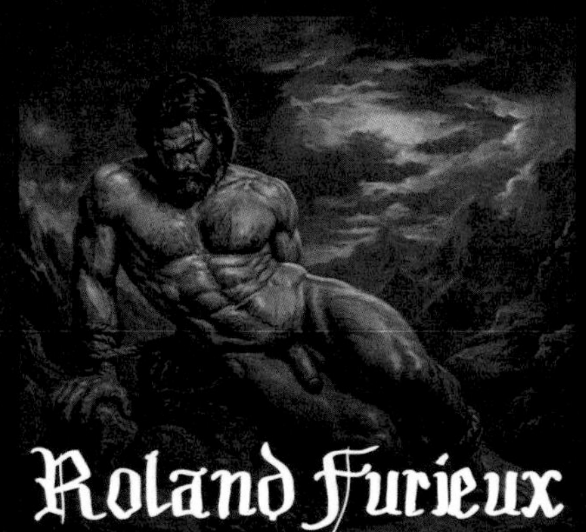

Roland Furieux

ASTRA ZERO INTERPRETATION OF
ROLAND FURIEUX,
BY JN DU SEIGNEUR, 1867

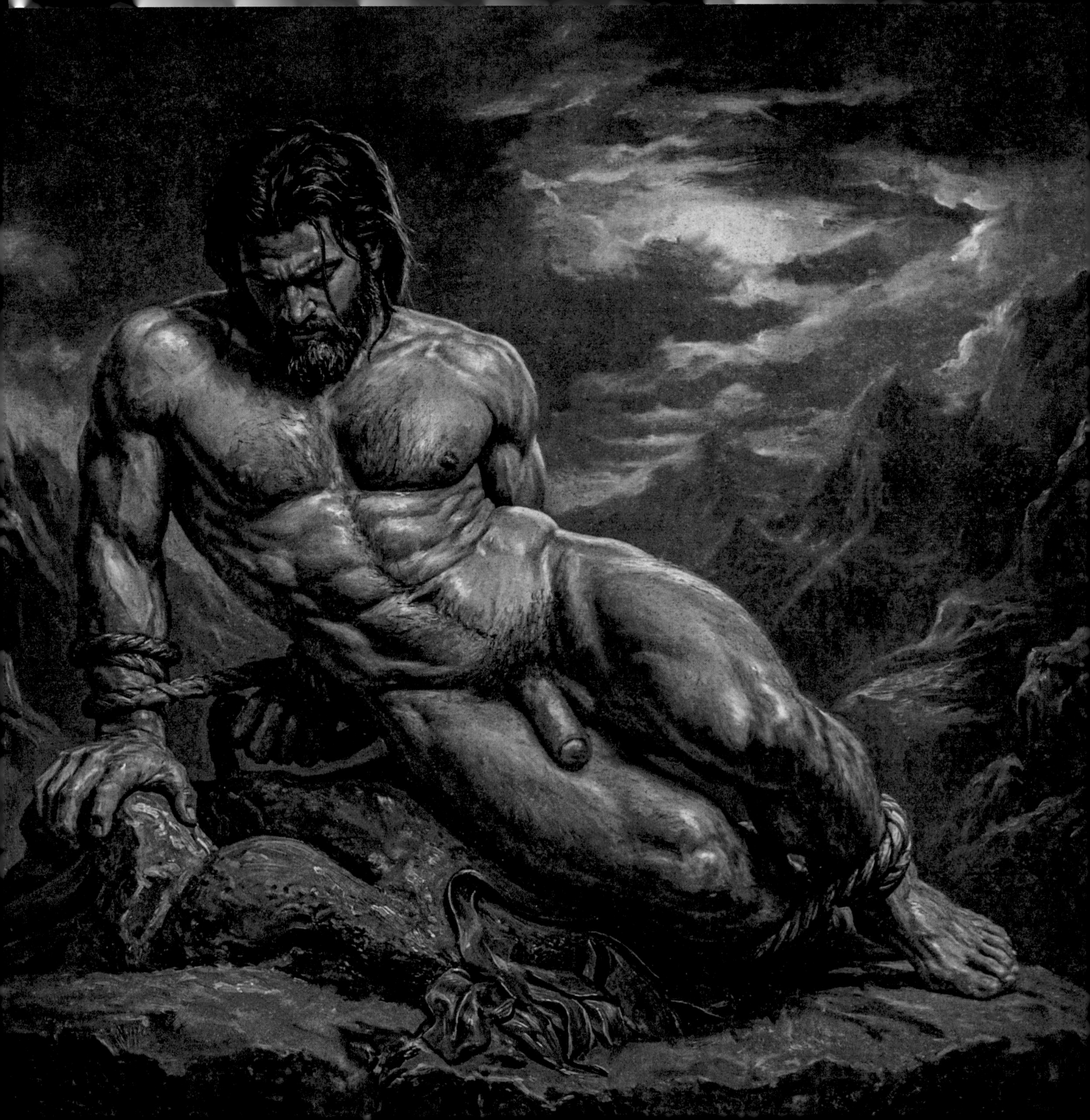

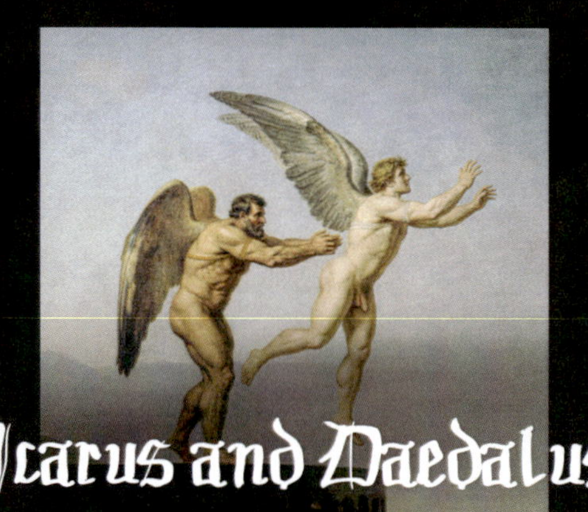

Icarus and Daedalus

ASTRA ZERO REVAMP OF,
ICARUS AND DAEDALUS, BY
CHARLES PAUL LANDON, 1799

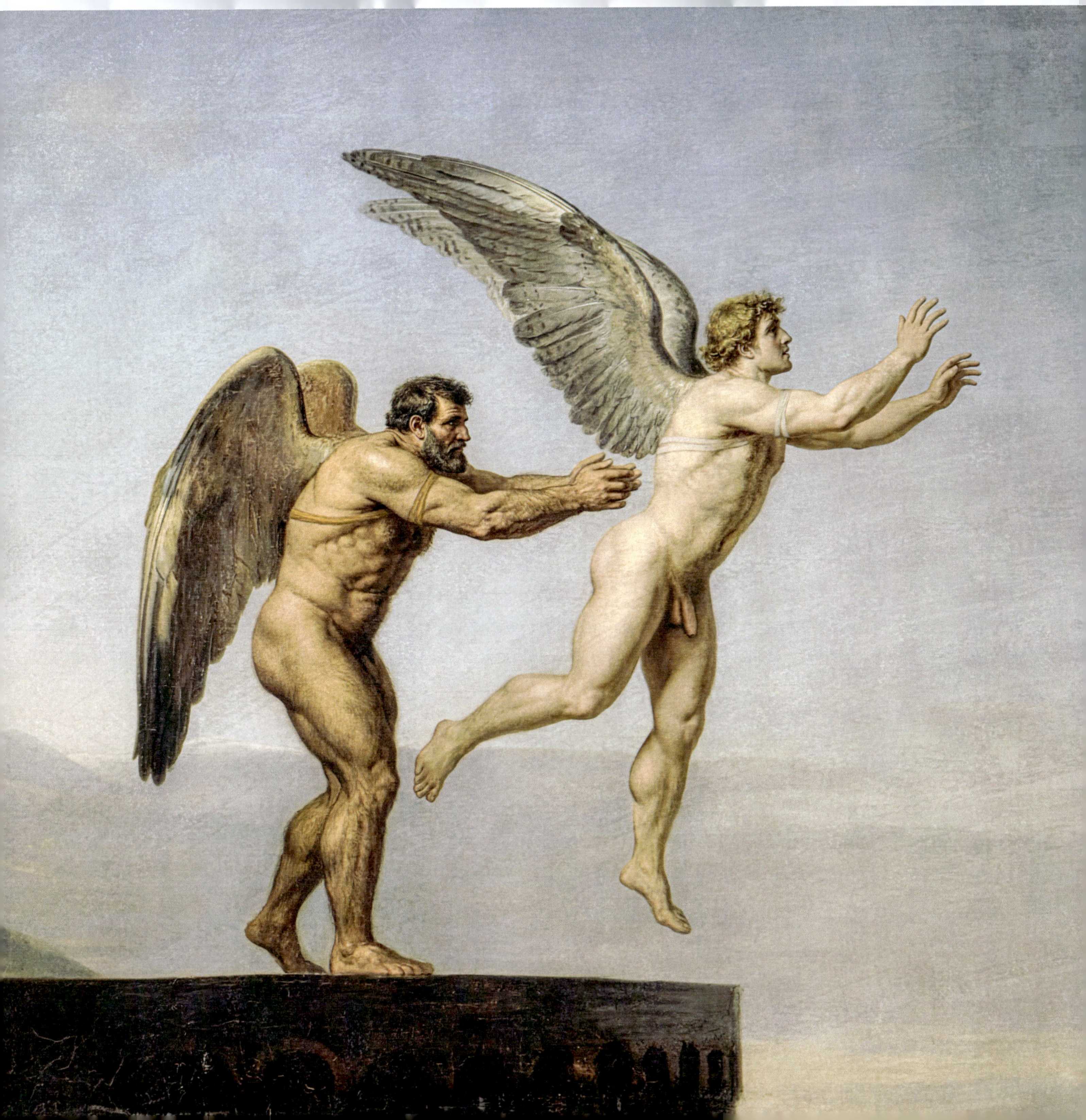

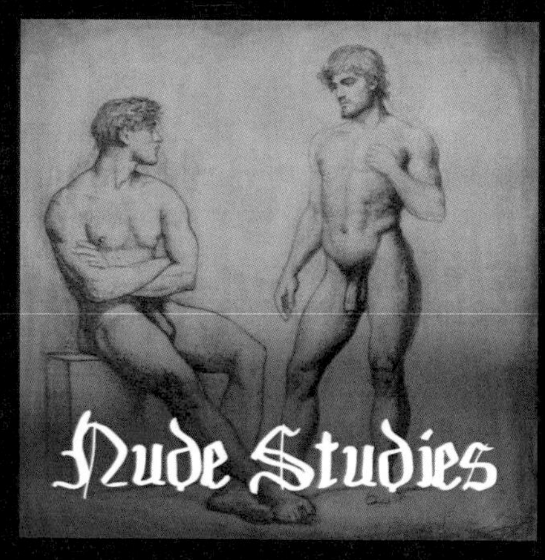

ASTRA ZERO REVAMP OF,
NUDE STUDIES, BY
GUSTAVE MOREAU, 1860

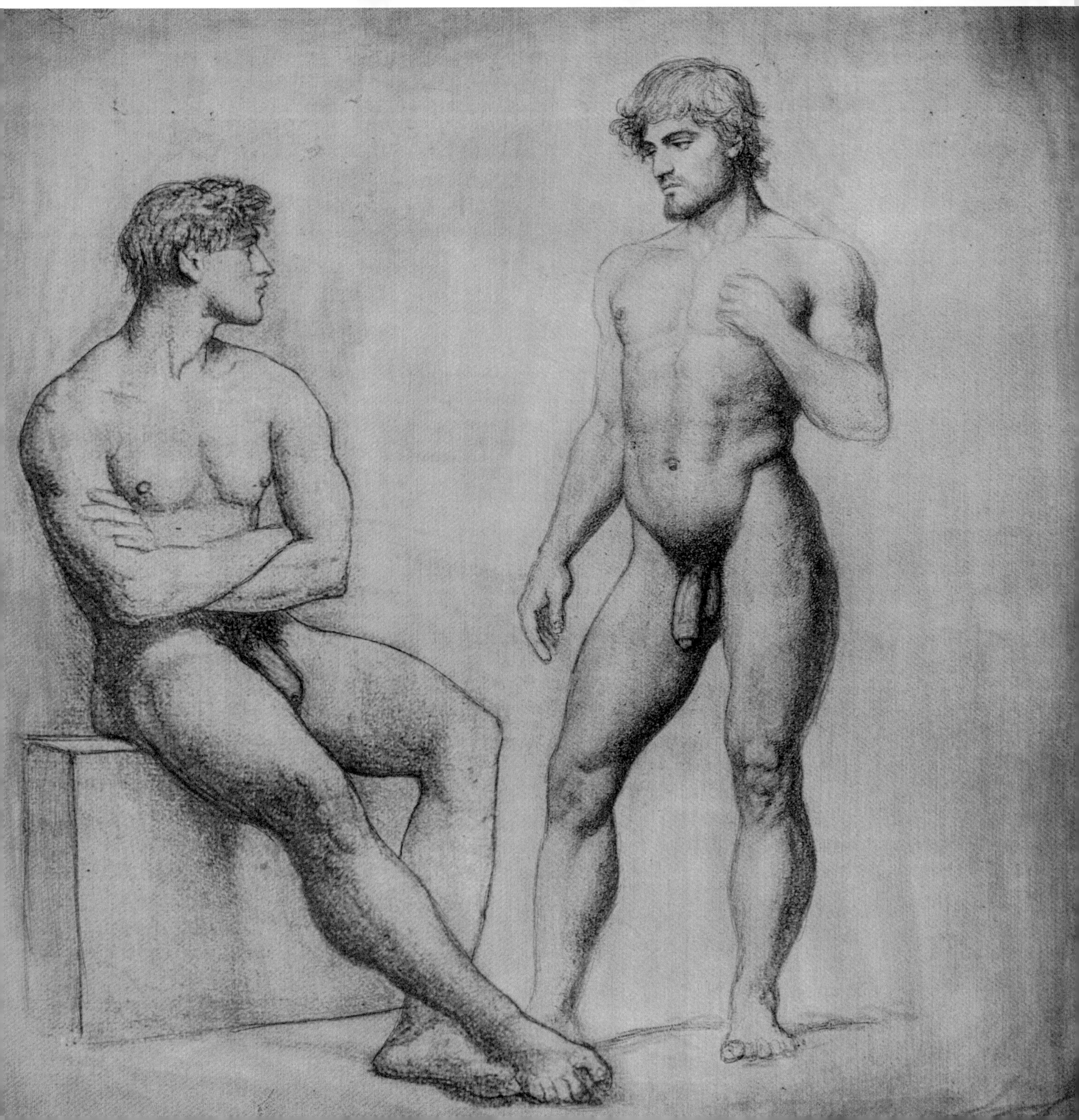

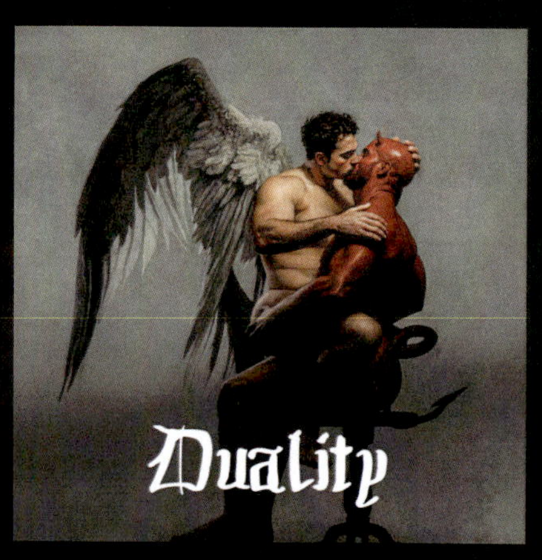

ASTRA ZERO ARTWORK INSPIRED BY
VARIOUS PAINTINGS
FROM 1800-1900

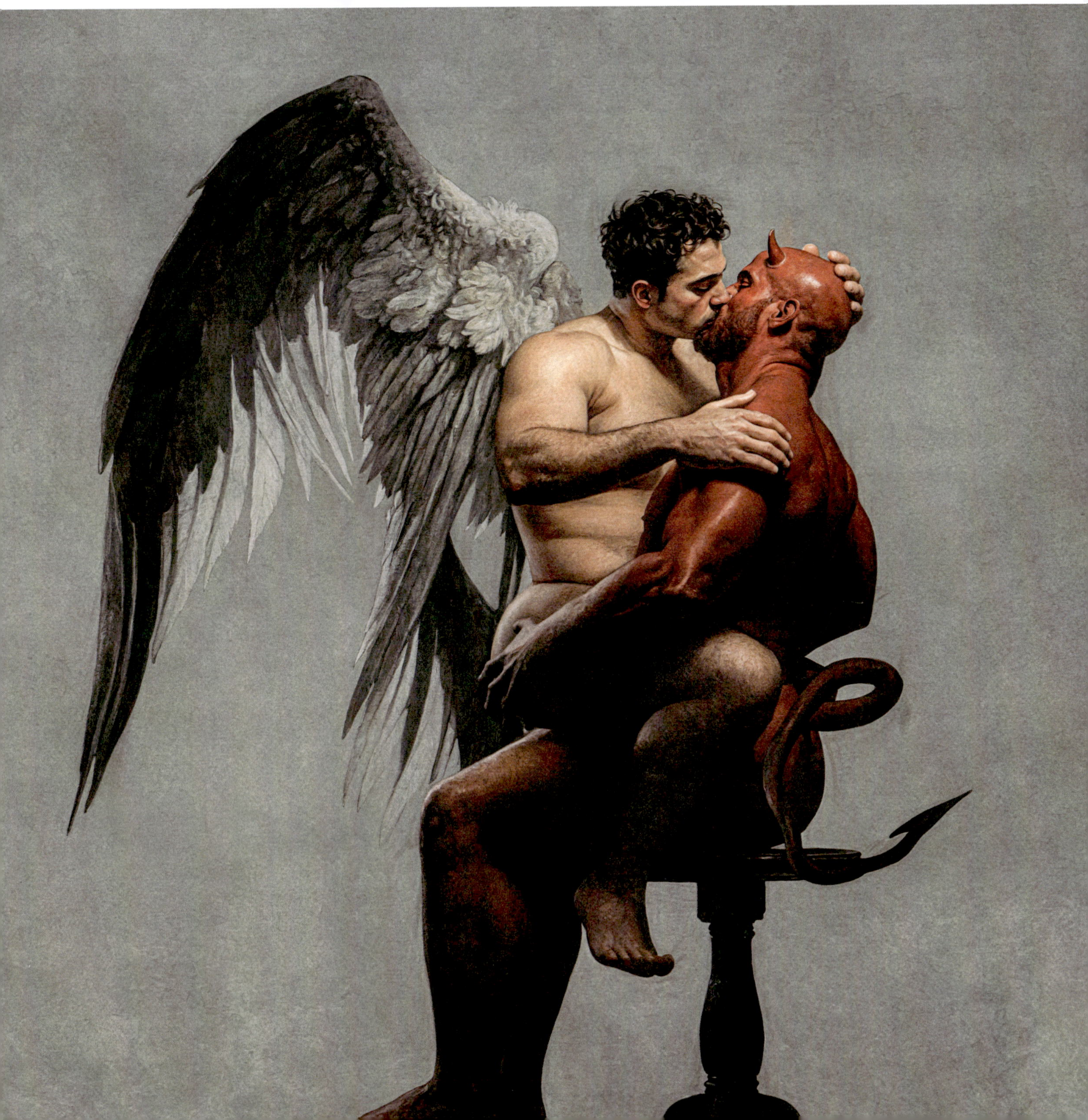

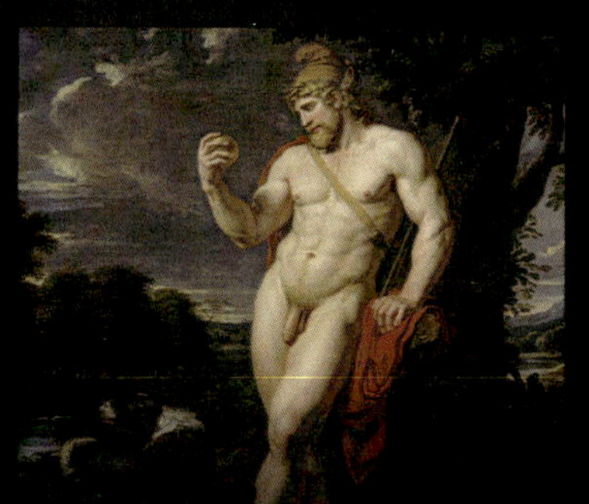

Le Berger Paris

ASTRA ZERO REVAMP OF,
LE BERGER PARIS, BY JEAN-BAPTISTE
FREDERIC DESMARAIS, 1787

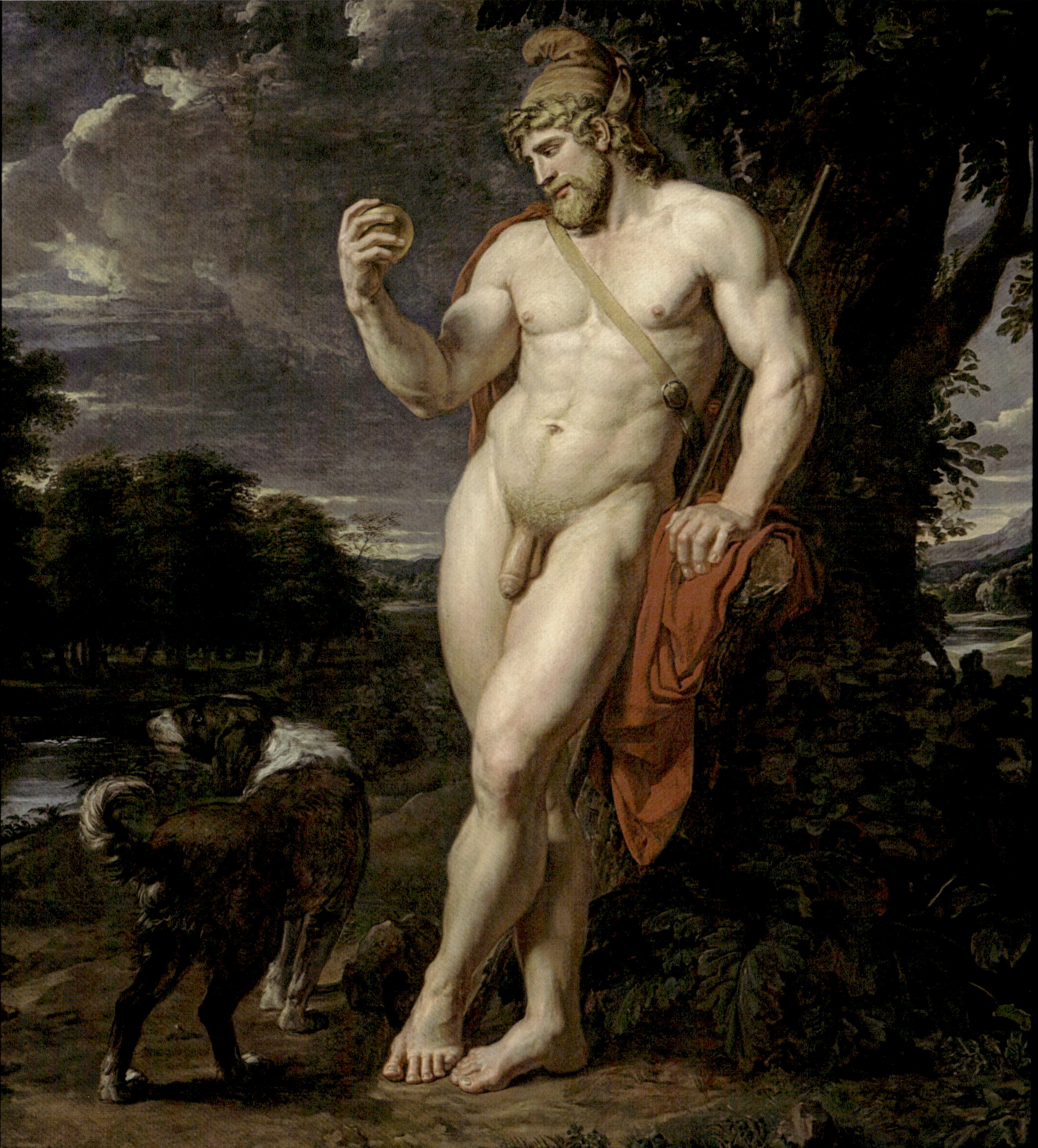

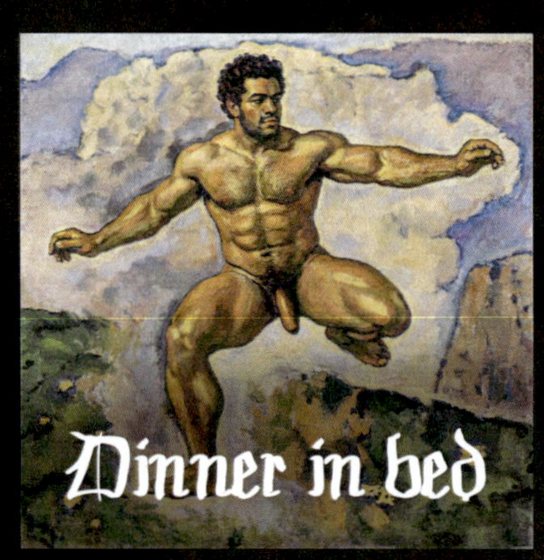

ASTRA ZERO REVAMP OF,
SPRING, BY KOLOMAN MOSER, 1900

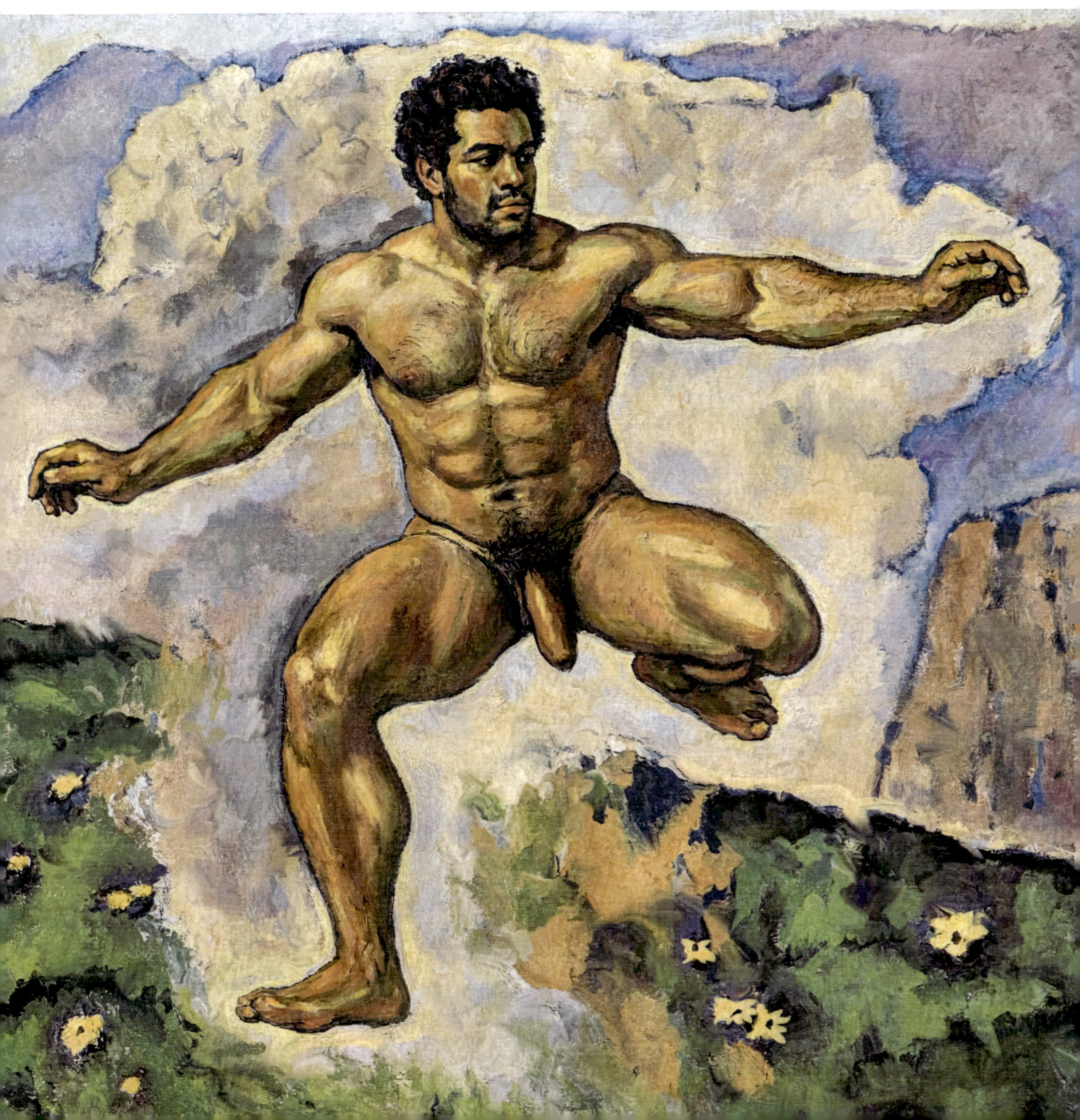

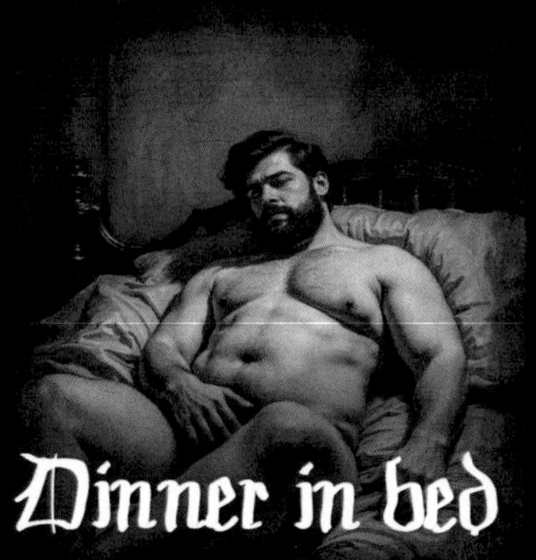

Dinner in bed

ASTRA ZERO REVAMP INSPIRED BY
VARIOUS PAINTINGS
FROM 1600-1800

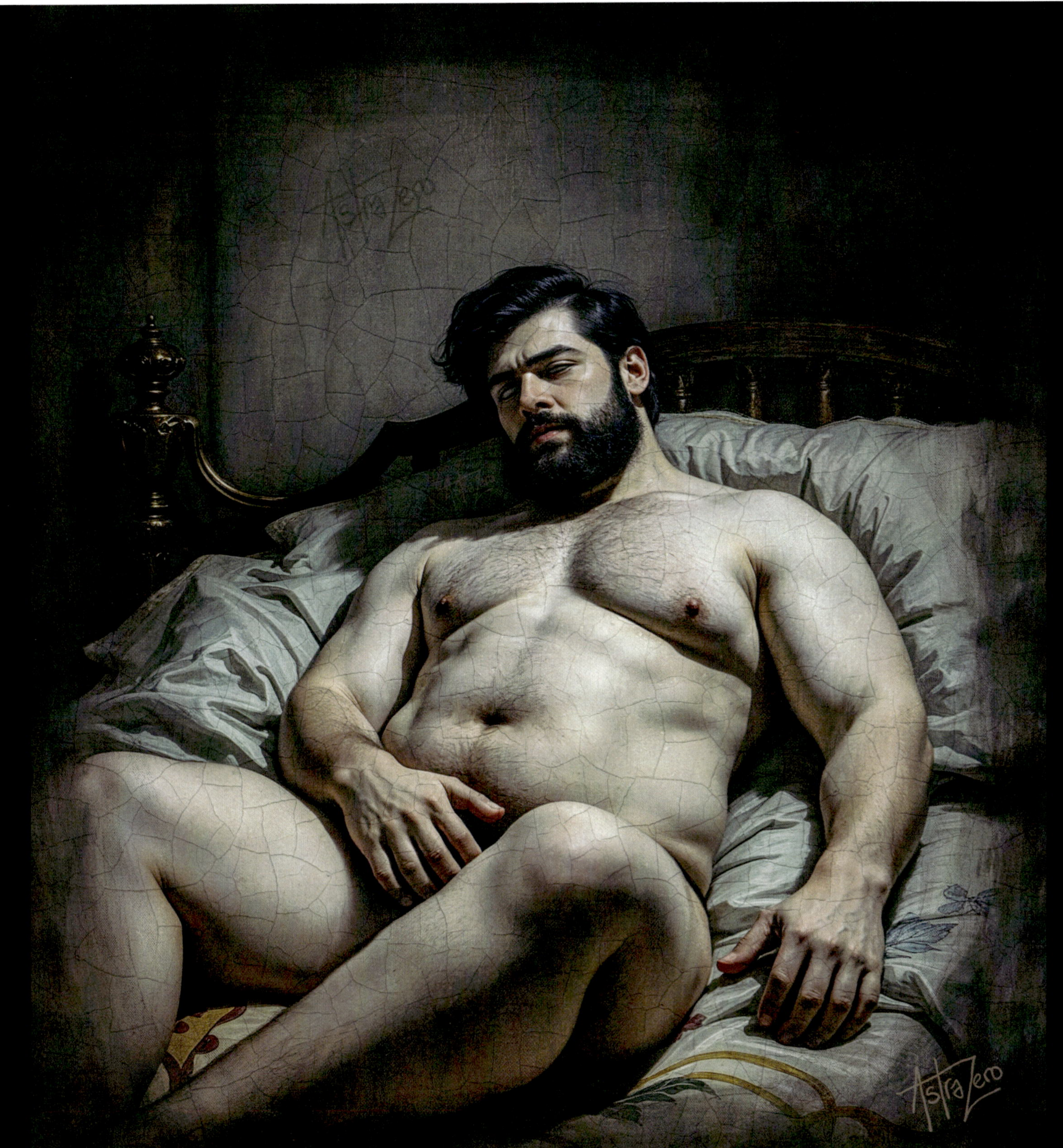

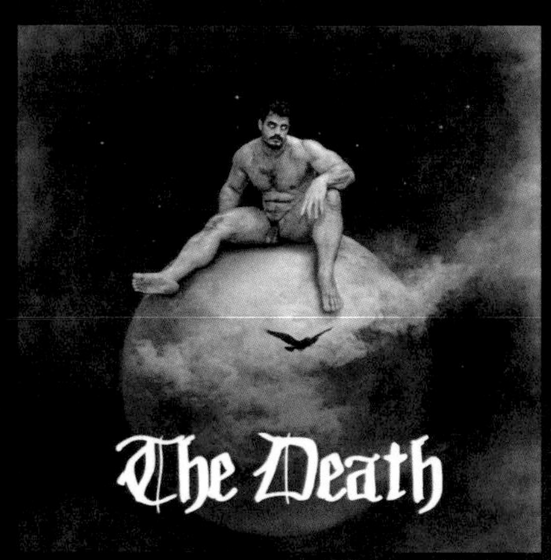

ASTRA ZERO REVAMP OF,
THE DEATH, BY
GUSTAVE DORE, 1883

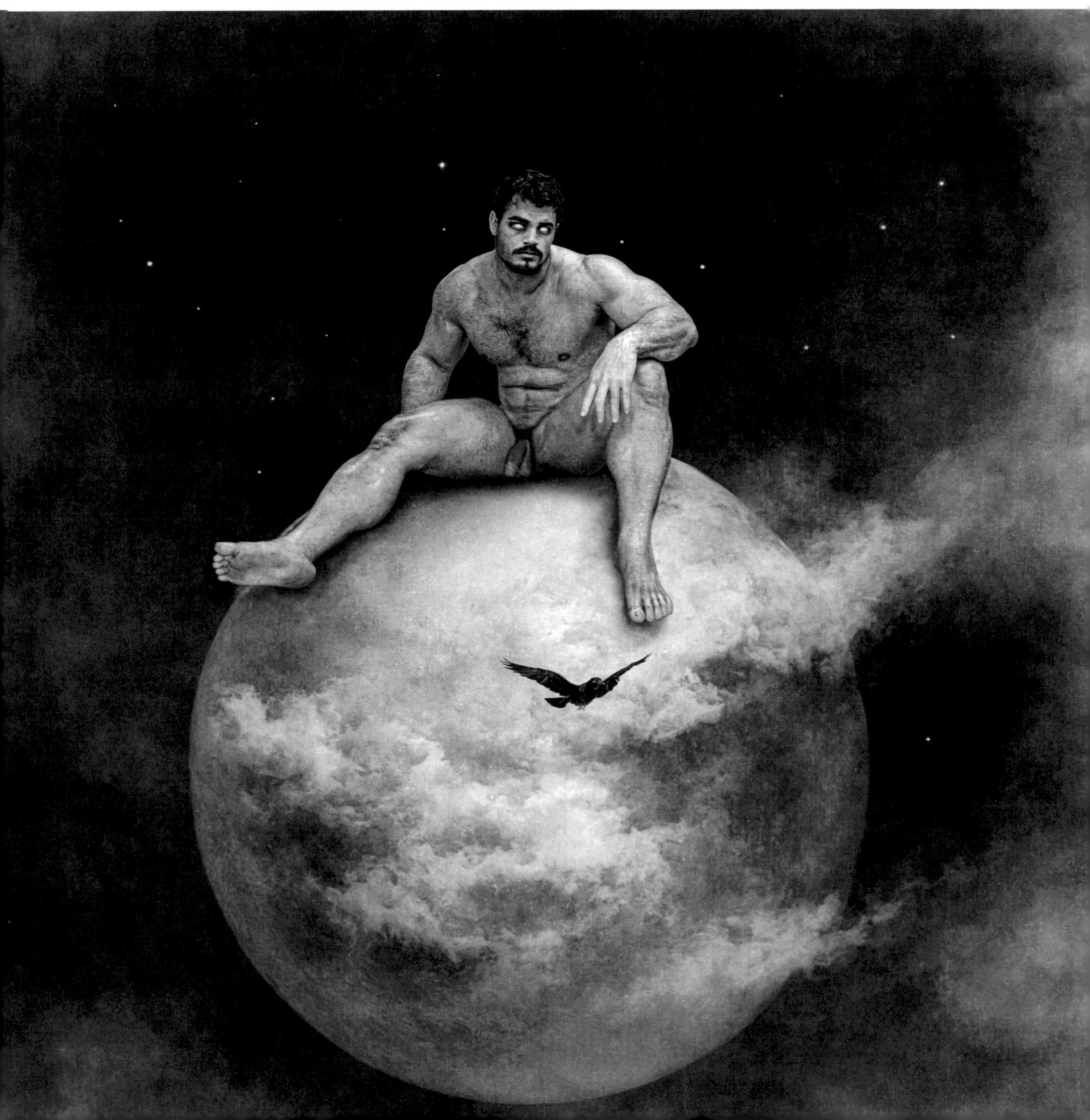

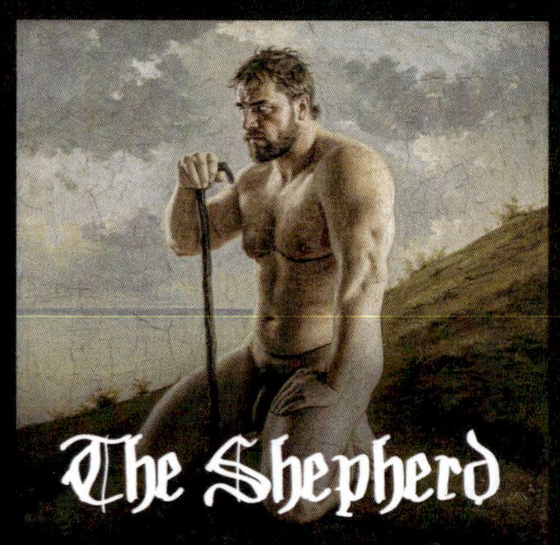

ASTRA ZERO REVAMP INSPIRED BY
VARIOUS PAINTINGS
FROM 1600-1800

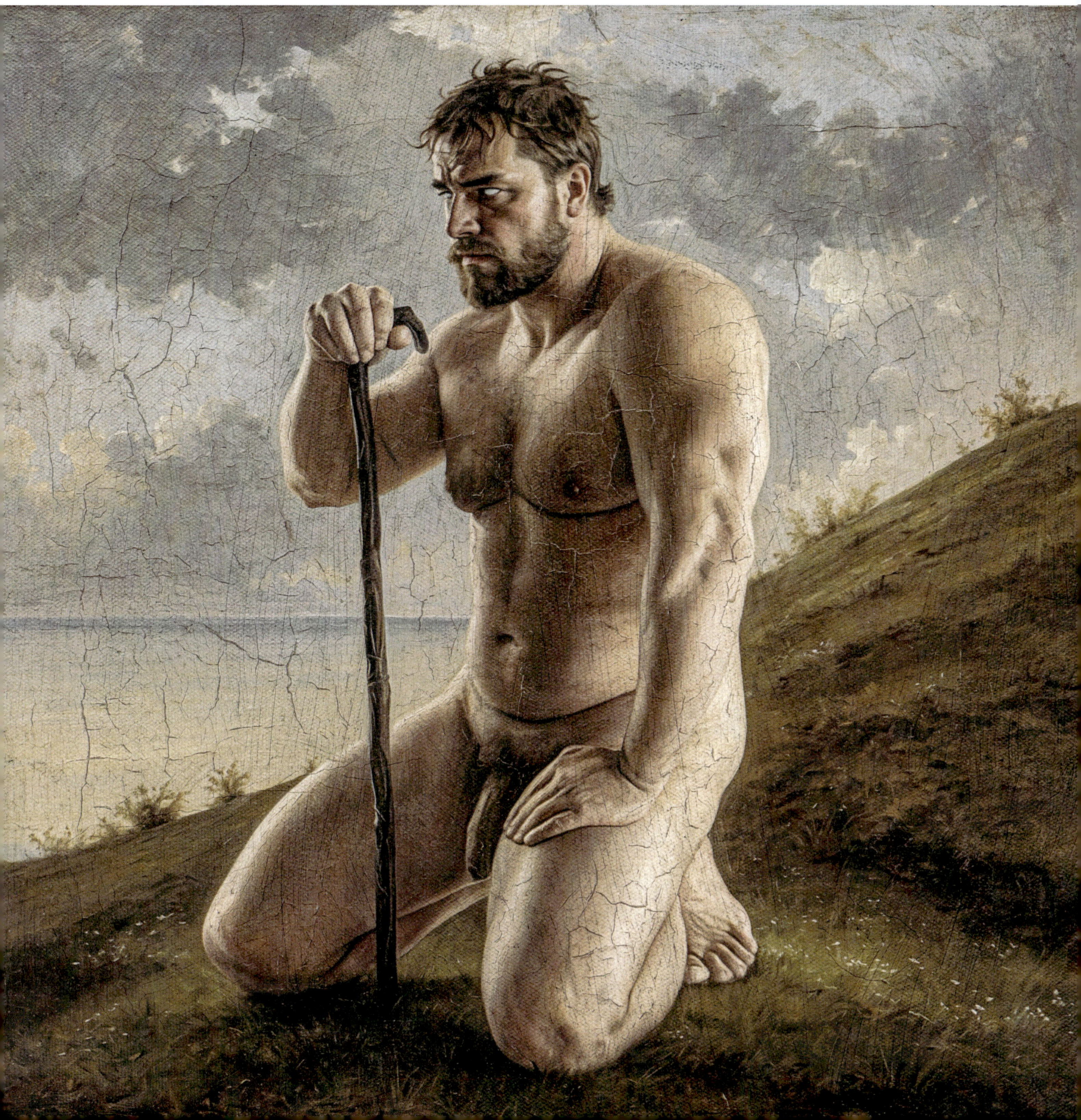

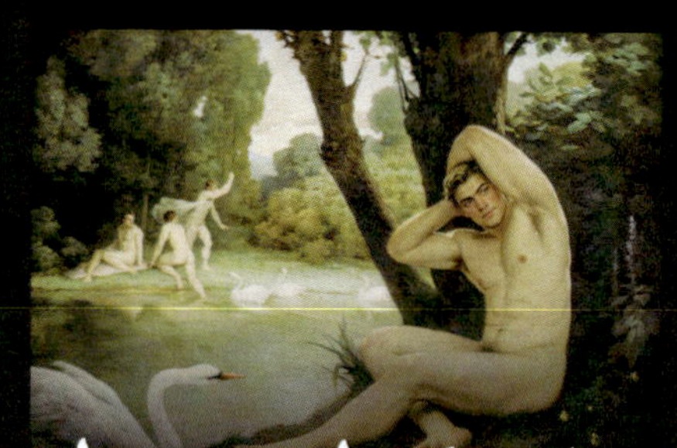

Lendan and the Swan

ASTRA ZERO REVAMP OF,
LEDA AND THE SWAN,
BY EMMANUEL BENNER, 1888

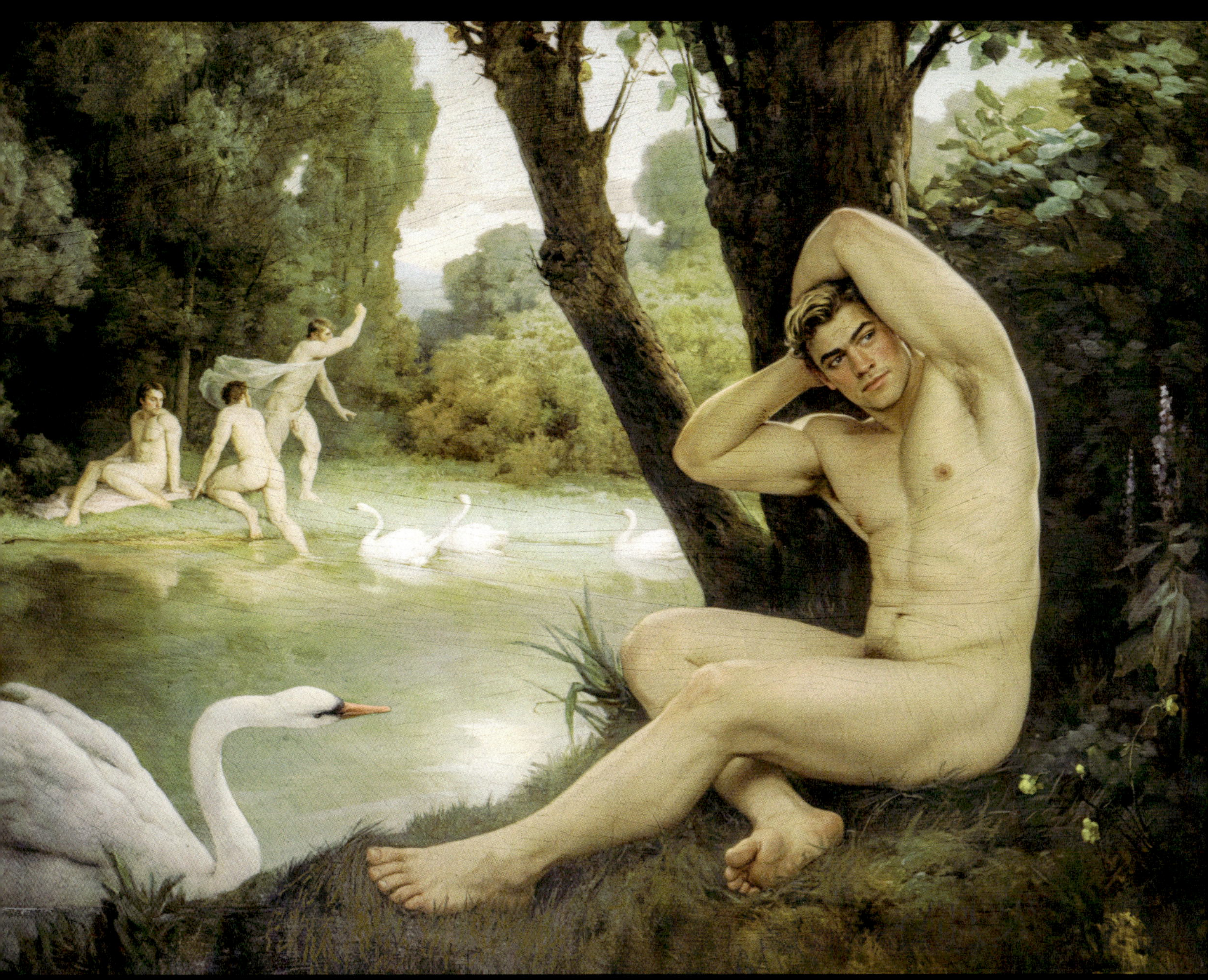

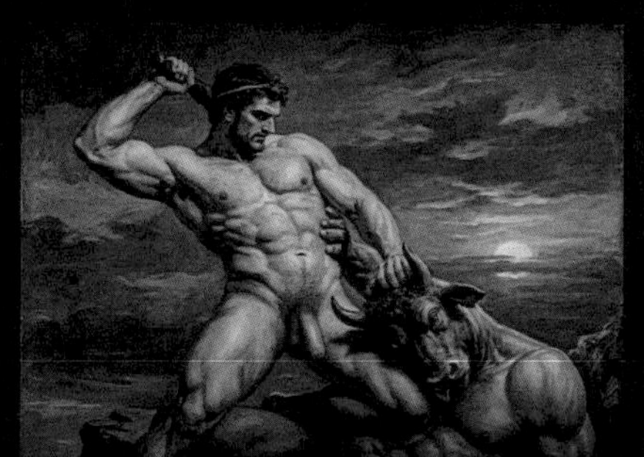

Theseus Fighting the Minotaur

ASTRA ZERO INTERPRETATION OF
THESEUS FIGHTING THE MINOTAUR,
BY JULES RAMEY, 1821

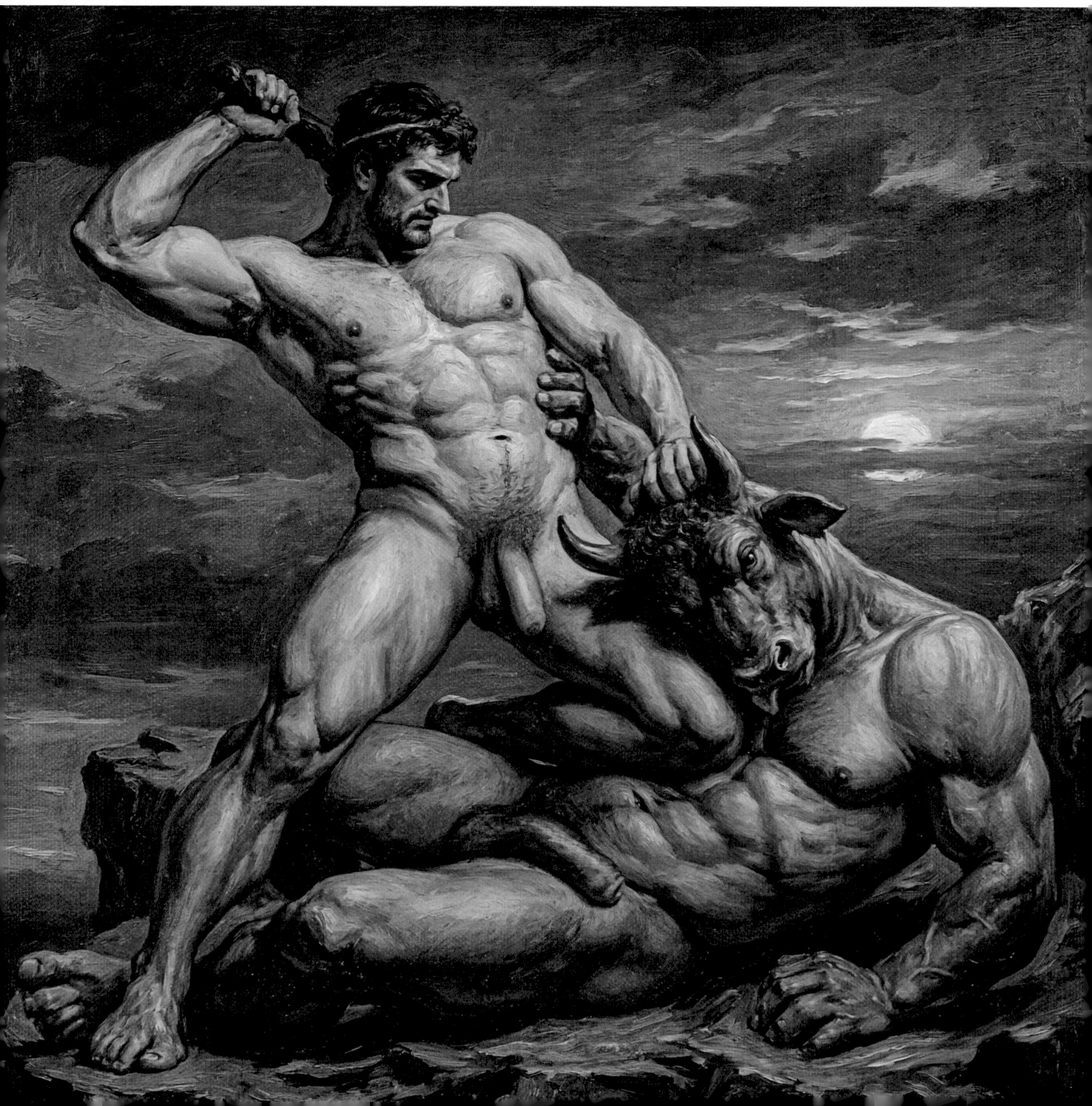

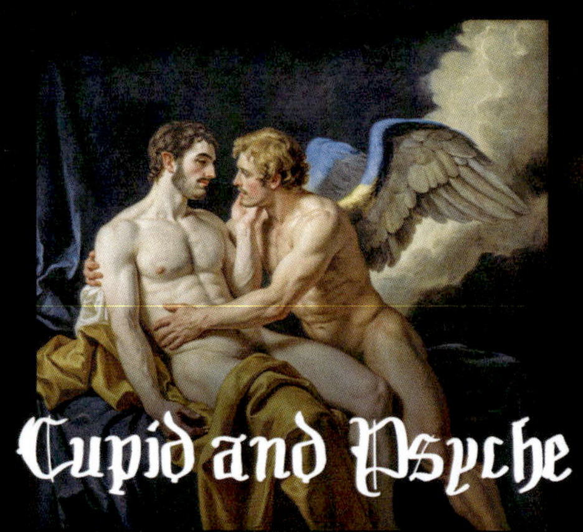

Cupid and Psyche

ASTRA ZERO REVAMP OF
CUPID AND PSYCHE,
BY LOUIS-JEAN-FRANCOIS LAGRENEE, 1767

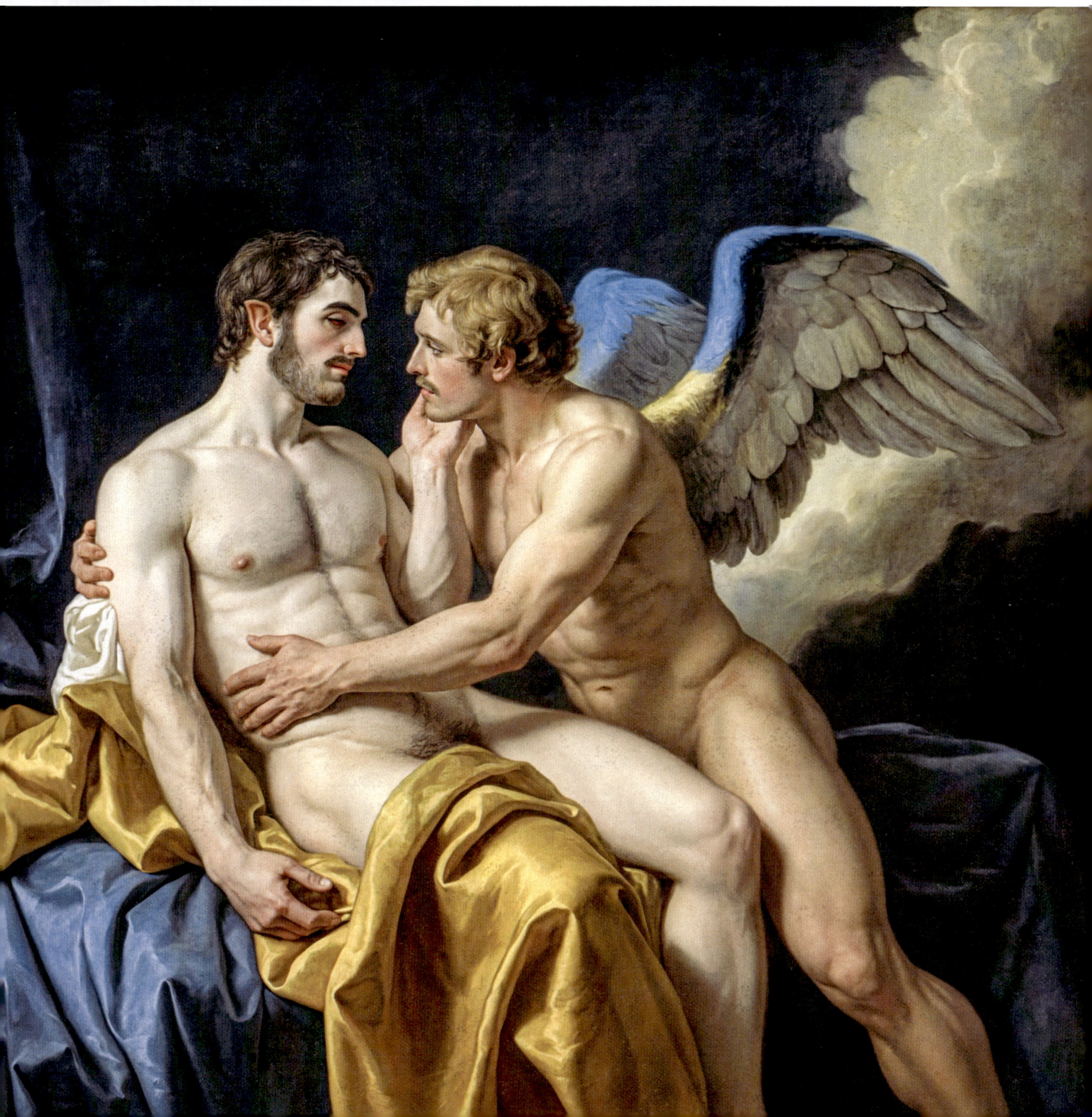

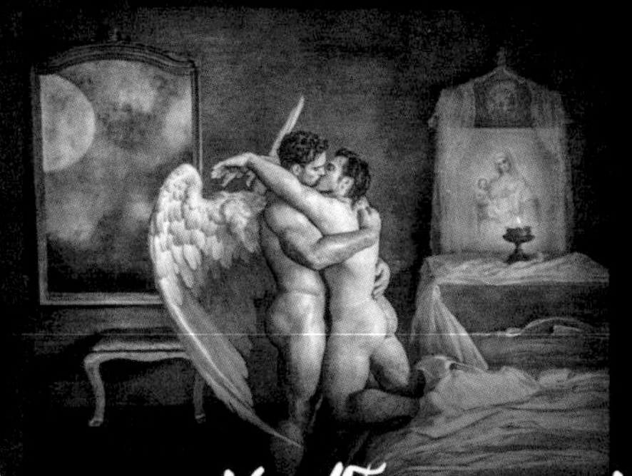

Romantic Encounter

ASTRA ZERO REVAMP OF
ROMANTIC ENCOUNTER,
BY MIHALY ZICHY, 1864

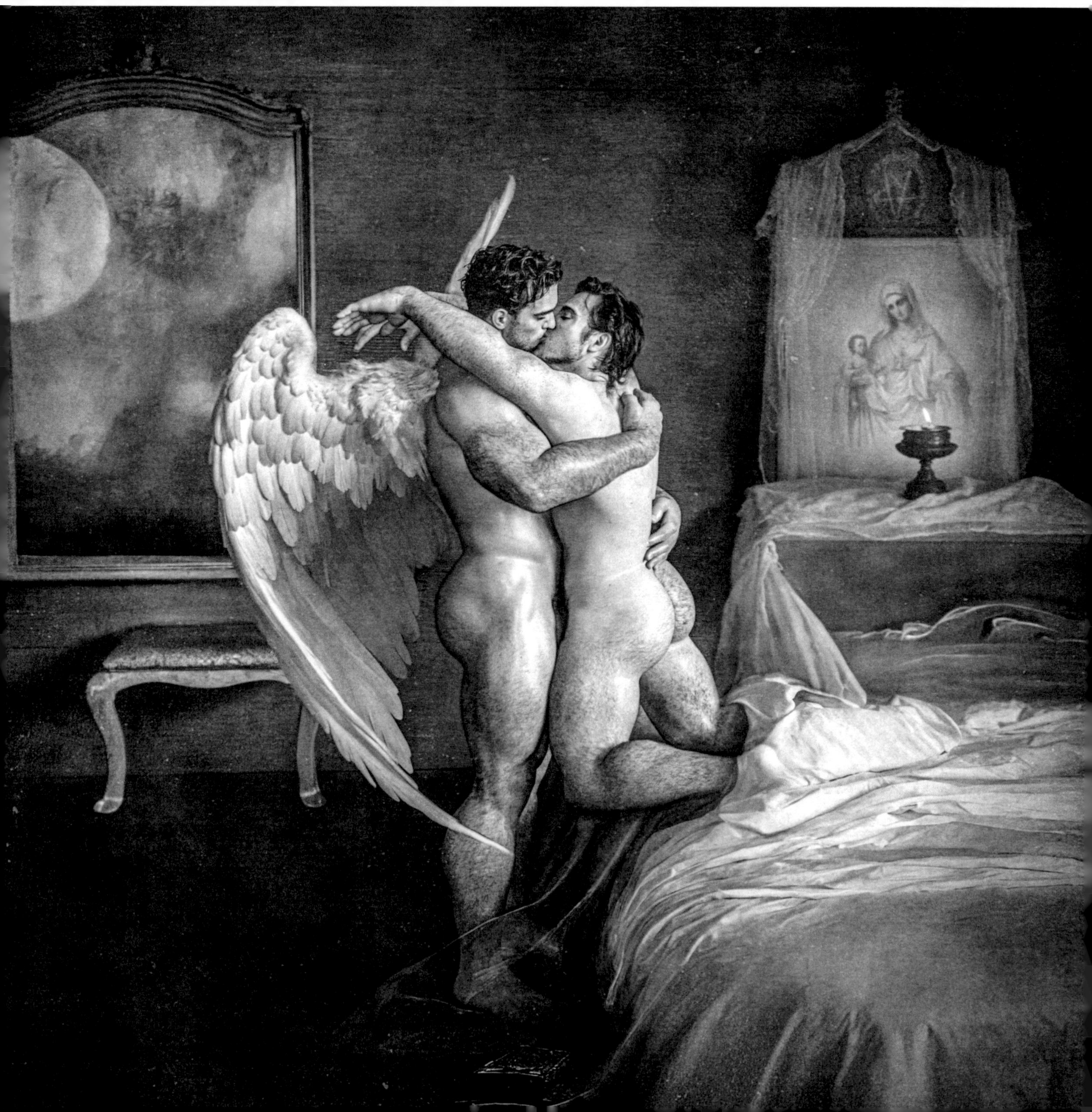

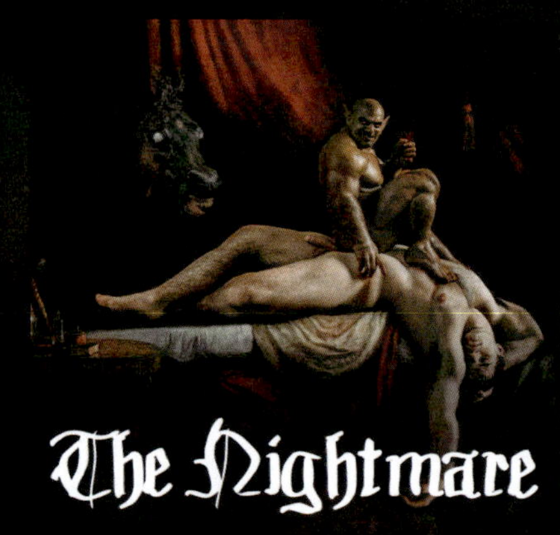

ASTRA ZERO REVAMP OF
THE NIGHTMARE,
BY HENRY FUSELI, 1781

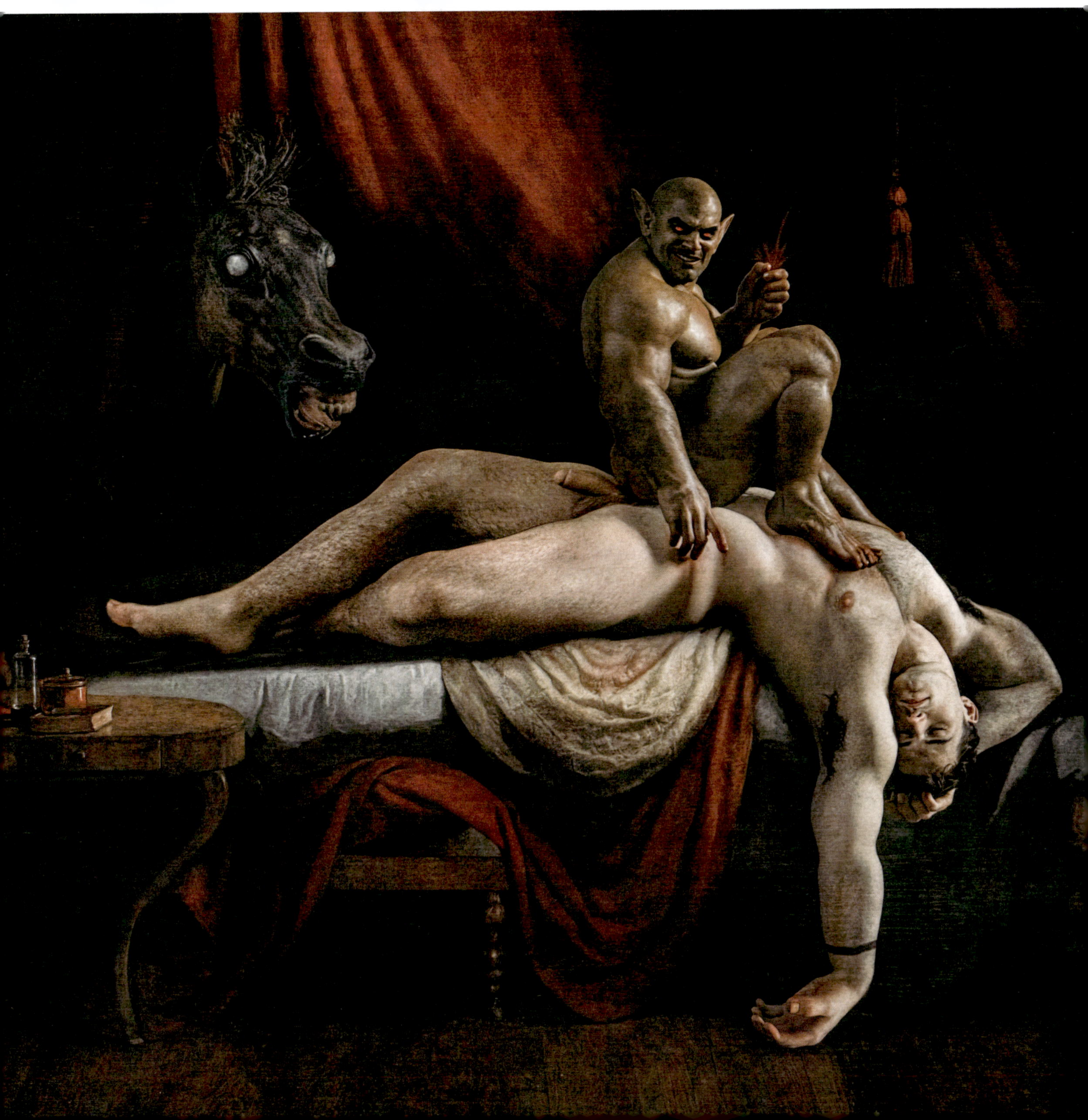

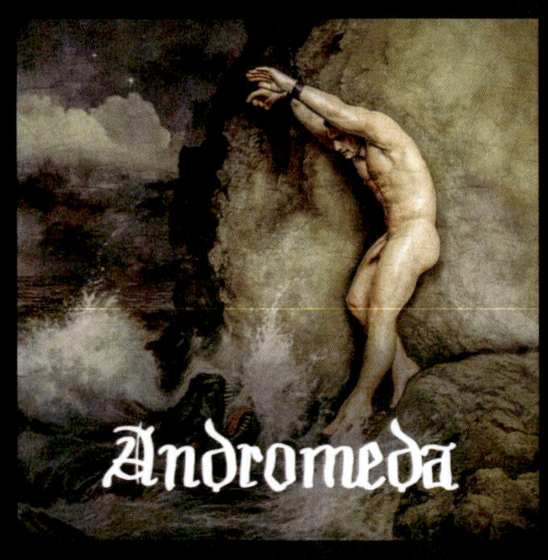

ASTRA ZERO REVAMP OF
ANDROMEDA, BY
GUSTAVE DORE, 1869

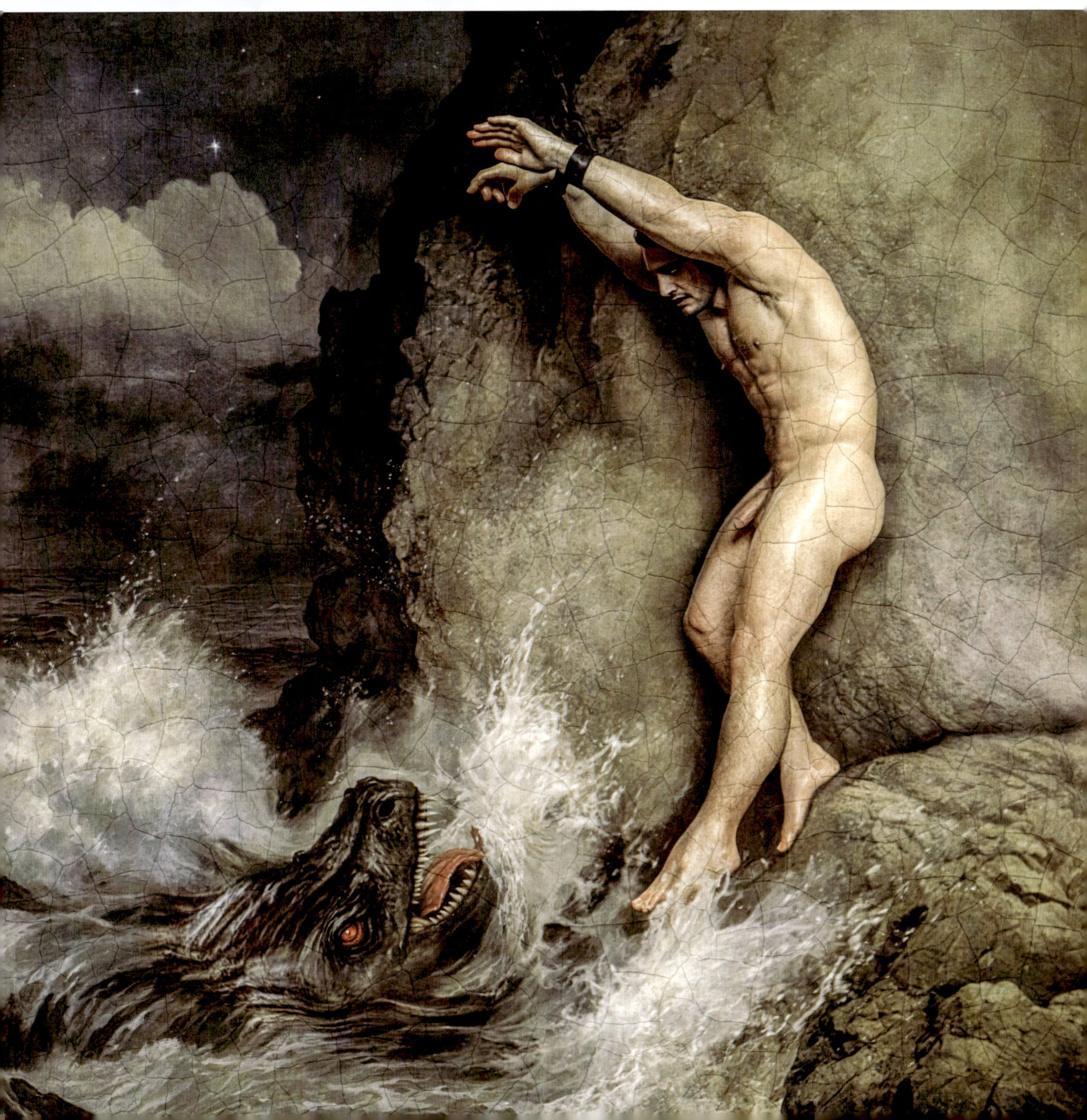

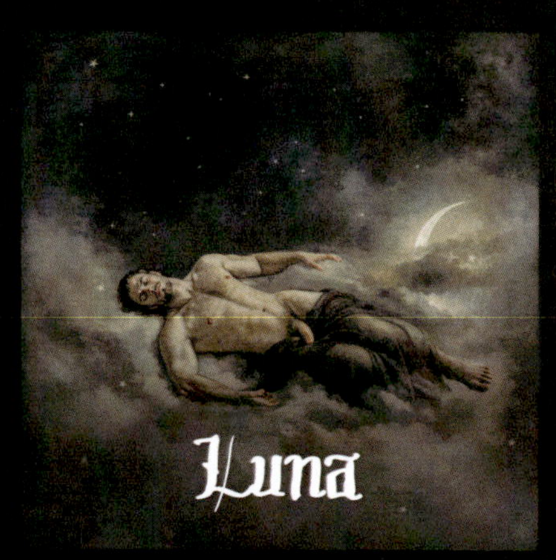

ASTRA ZERO REVAMP OF
LUNA, BY
LEON-FRANCOIS COMERRE, 1850-1916

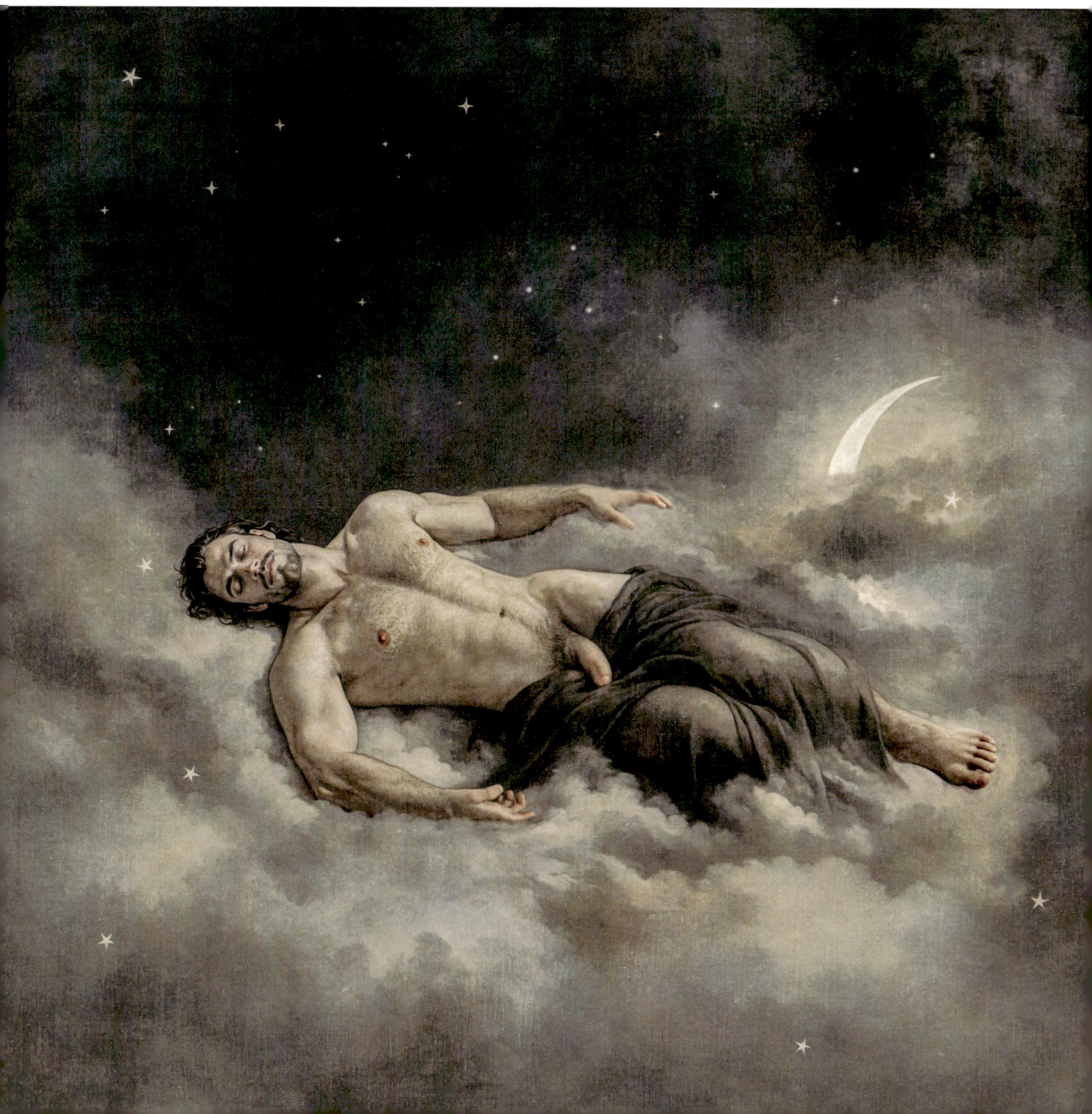

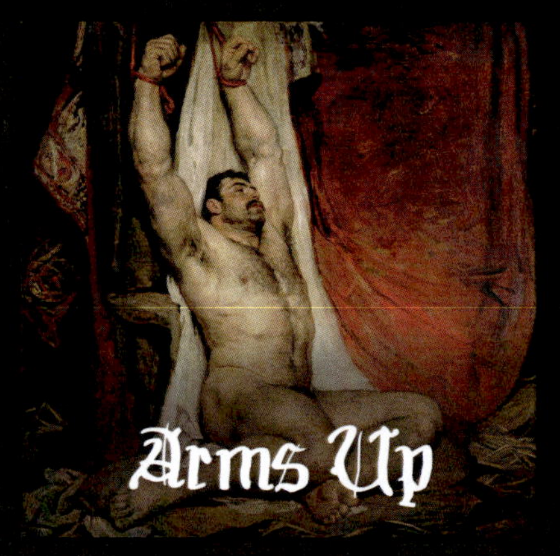

ASTRA ZERO REVAMP OF
MALE WITH ARMS UP-STRETCHED BY
WILLIAM ETTY , 1828

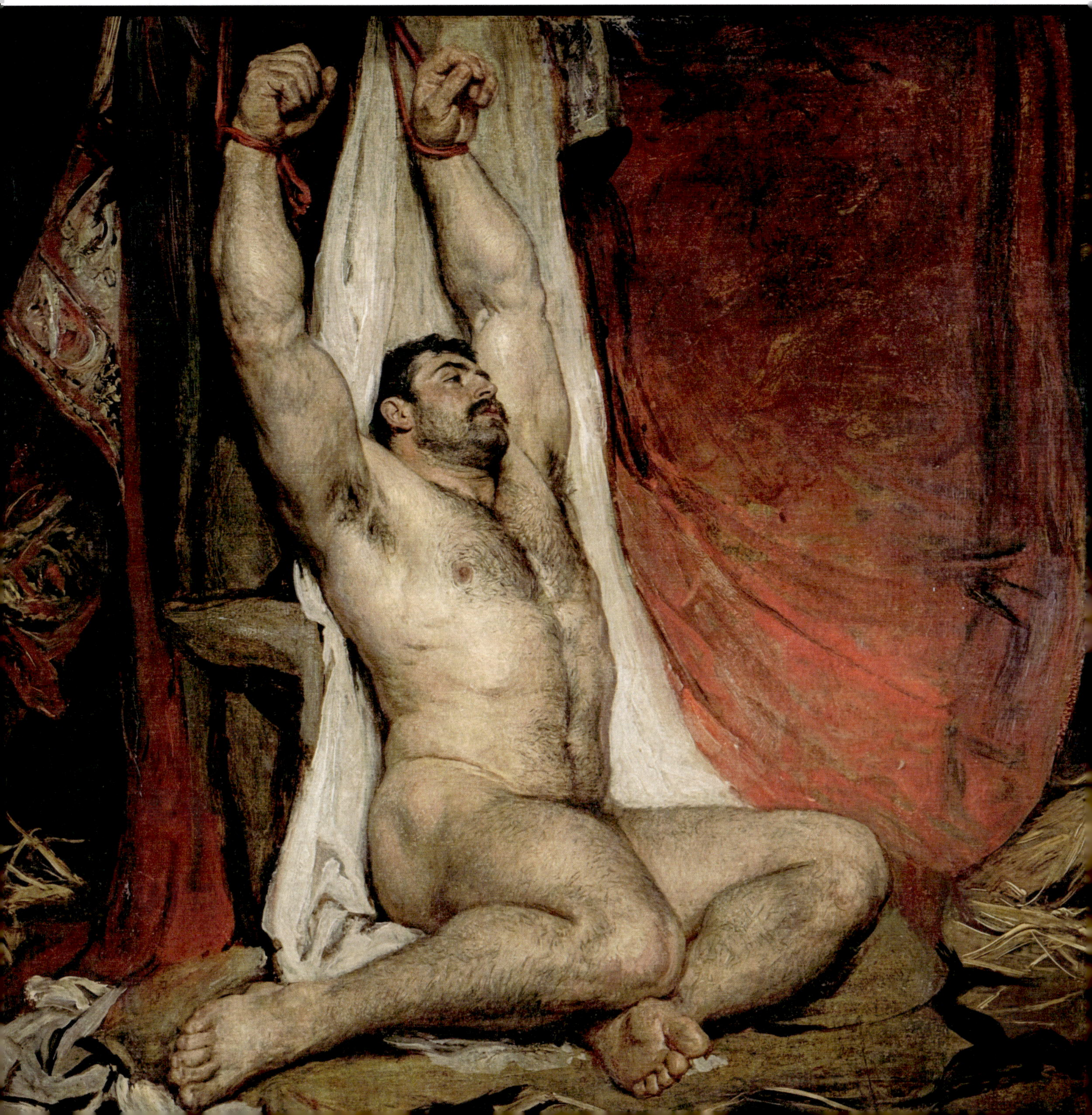

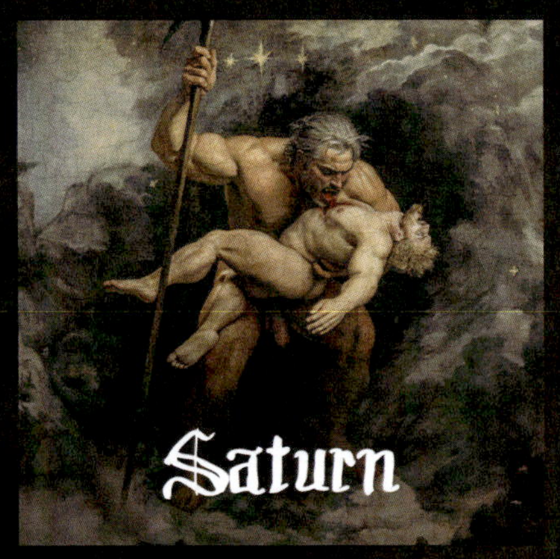

ASTRA ZERO REVAMP OF
SATURN, BY
PETER PAUL RUBENS, 1636

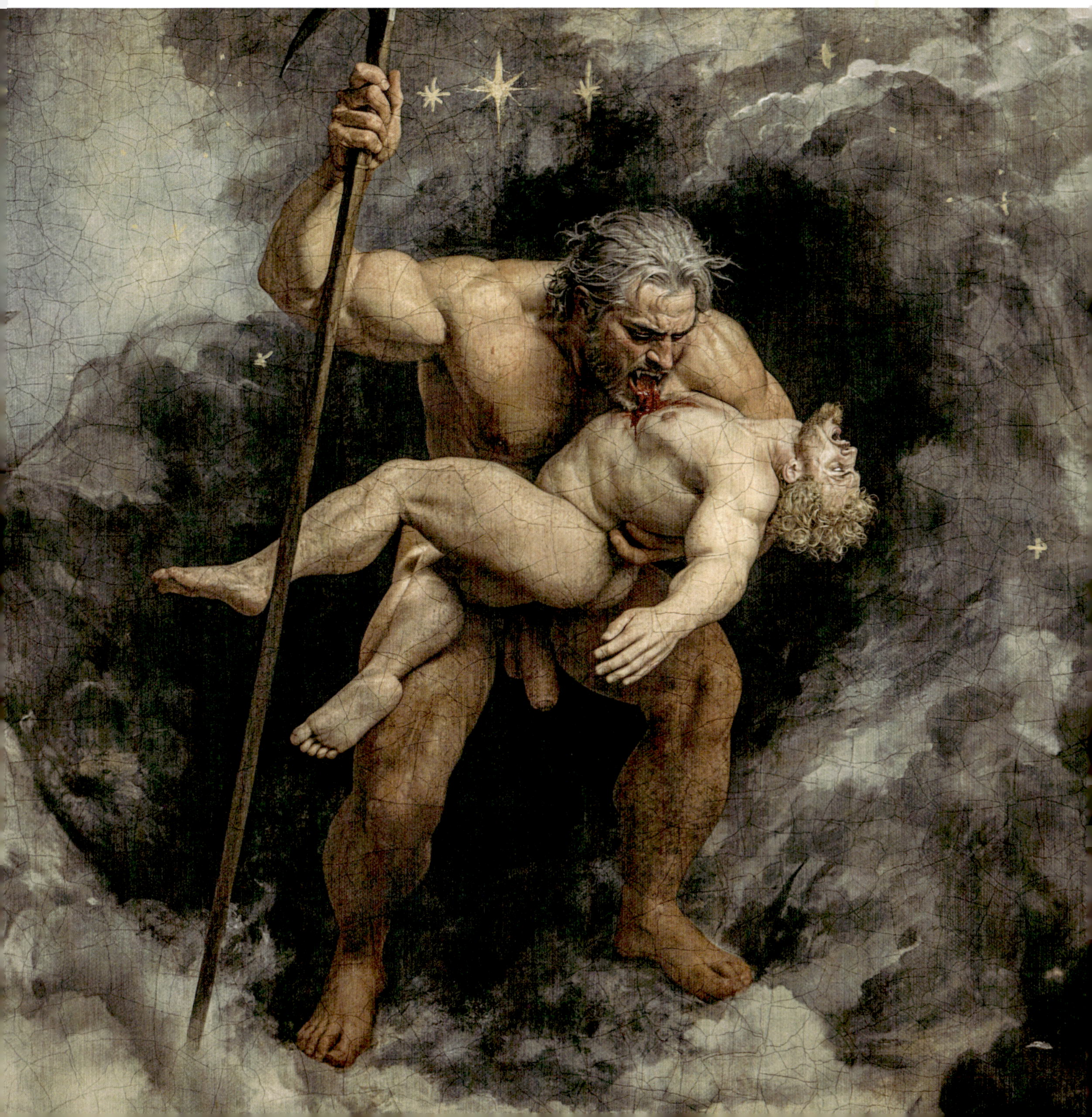

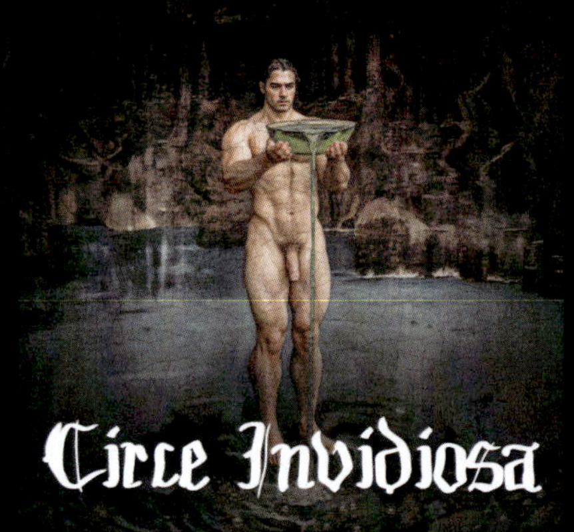

ASTRA ZERO REVAMP OF
CIRCE INVIDIOSA BY
JOHN WILLIAM WATERHOUSE, 1892

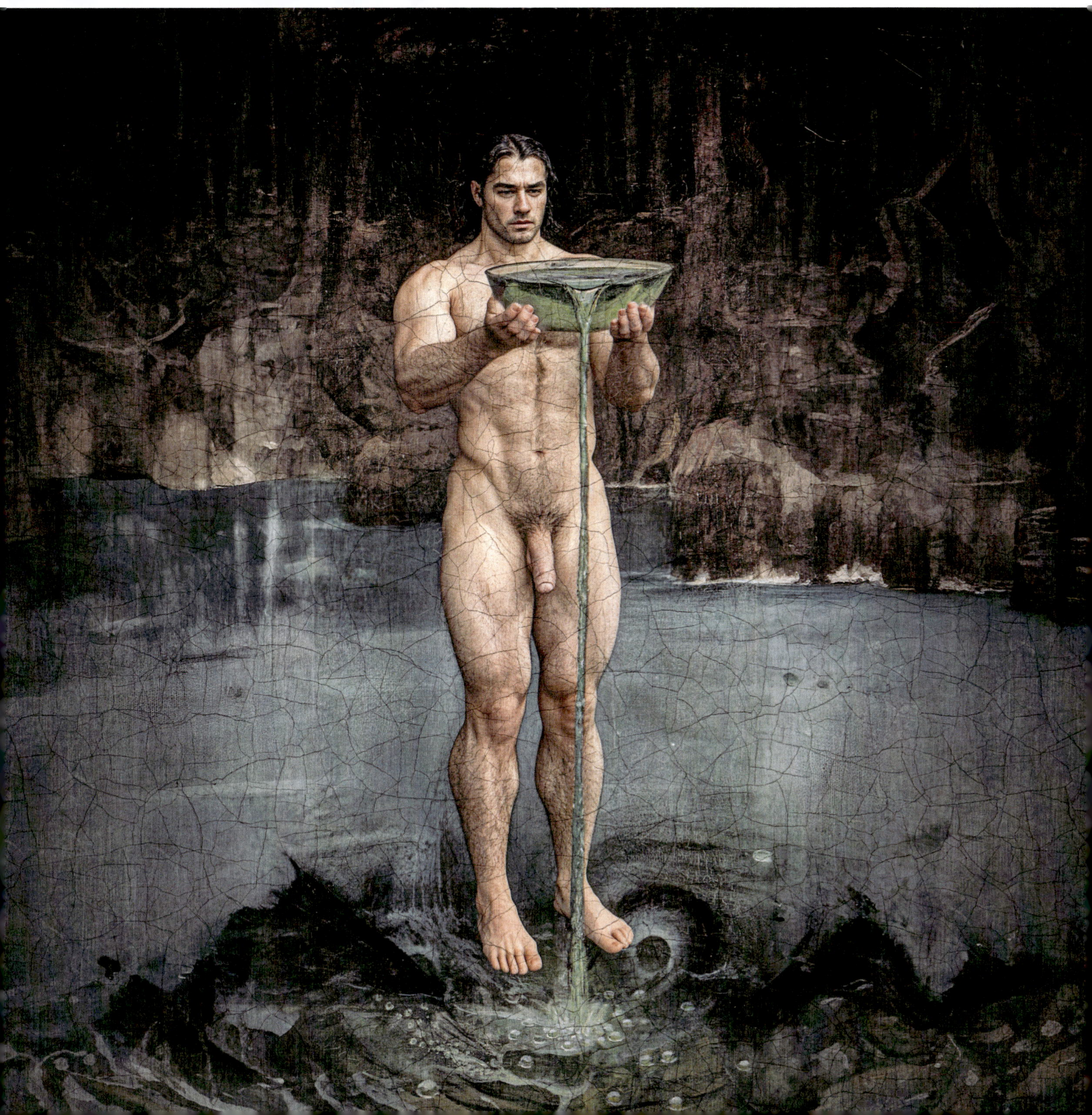

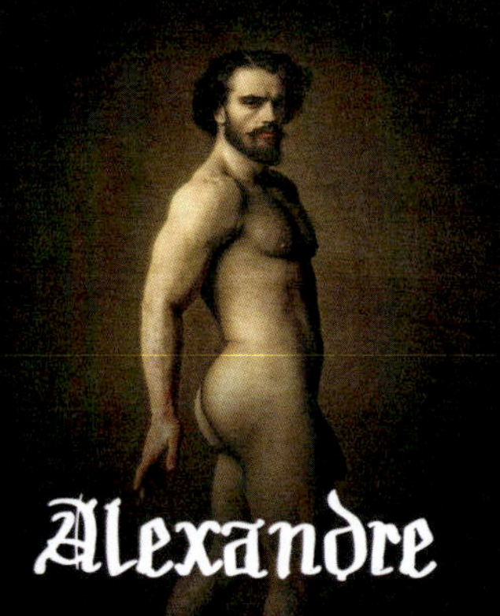

Alexandre

ASTRA ZERO REVAMP OF
SELF-PORTRAIT, BY
ALEXANDRE CABANEL, 1852

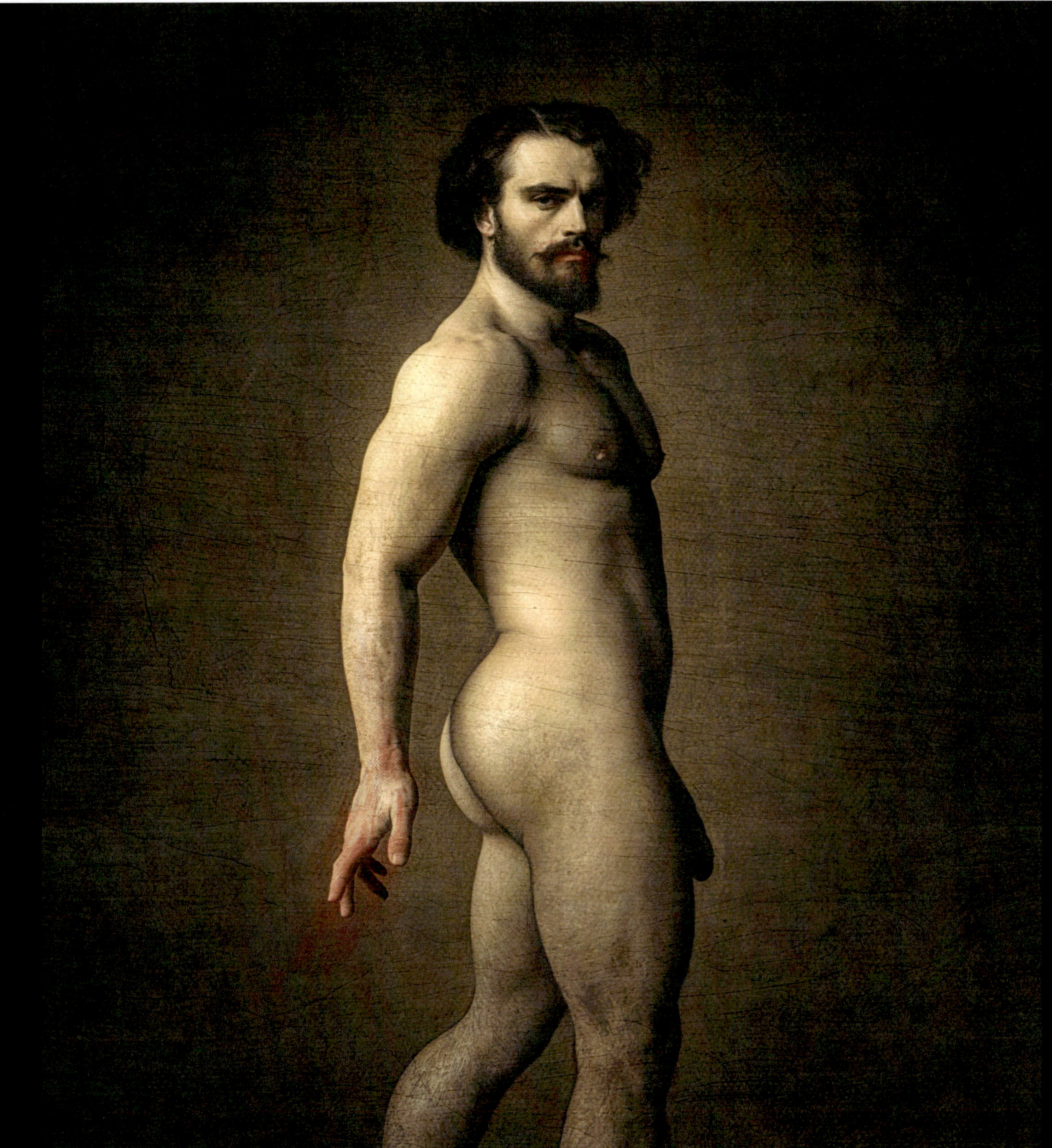

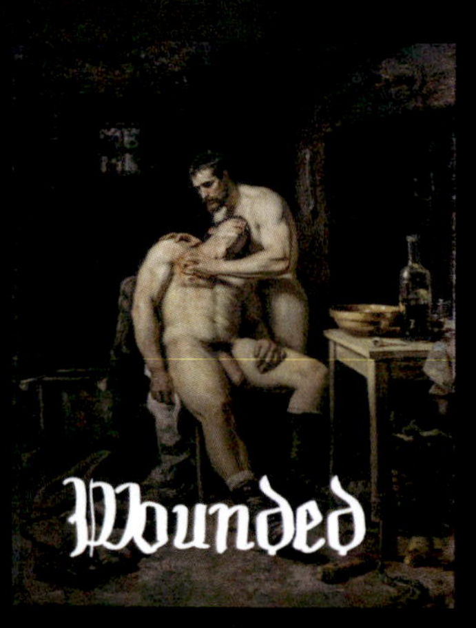

ASTRA ZERO REVAMP OF
LE RETOUR DU BRACONNIER,
BY HENRY JONES THADDEUS, 1881

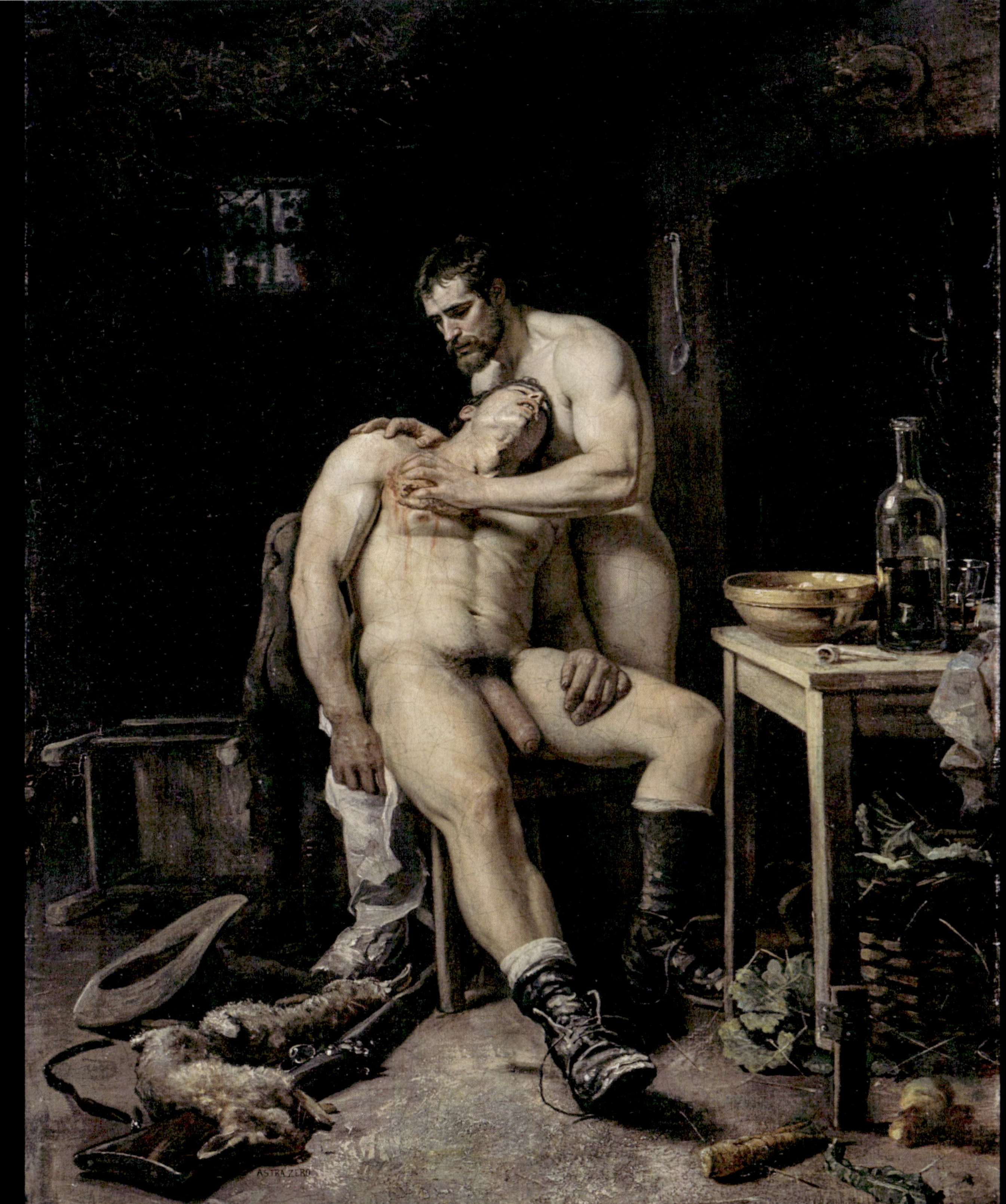

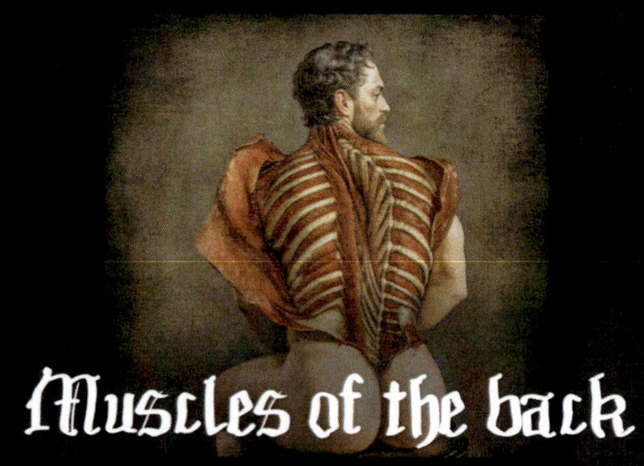

Muscles of the back

ASTRA ZERO REVAMP OF
MUSCLES OF THE BACK BY
J.F. GAUTIER D'AGOTY, 1745/1746

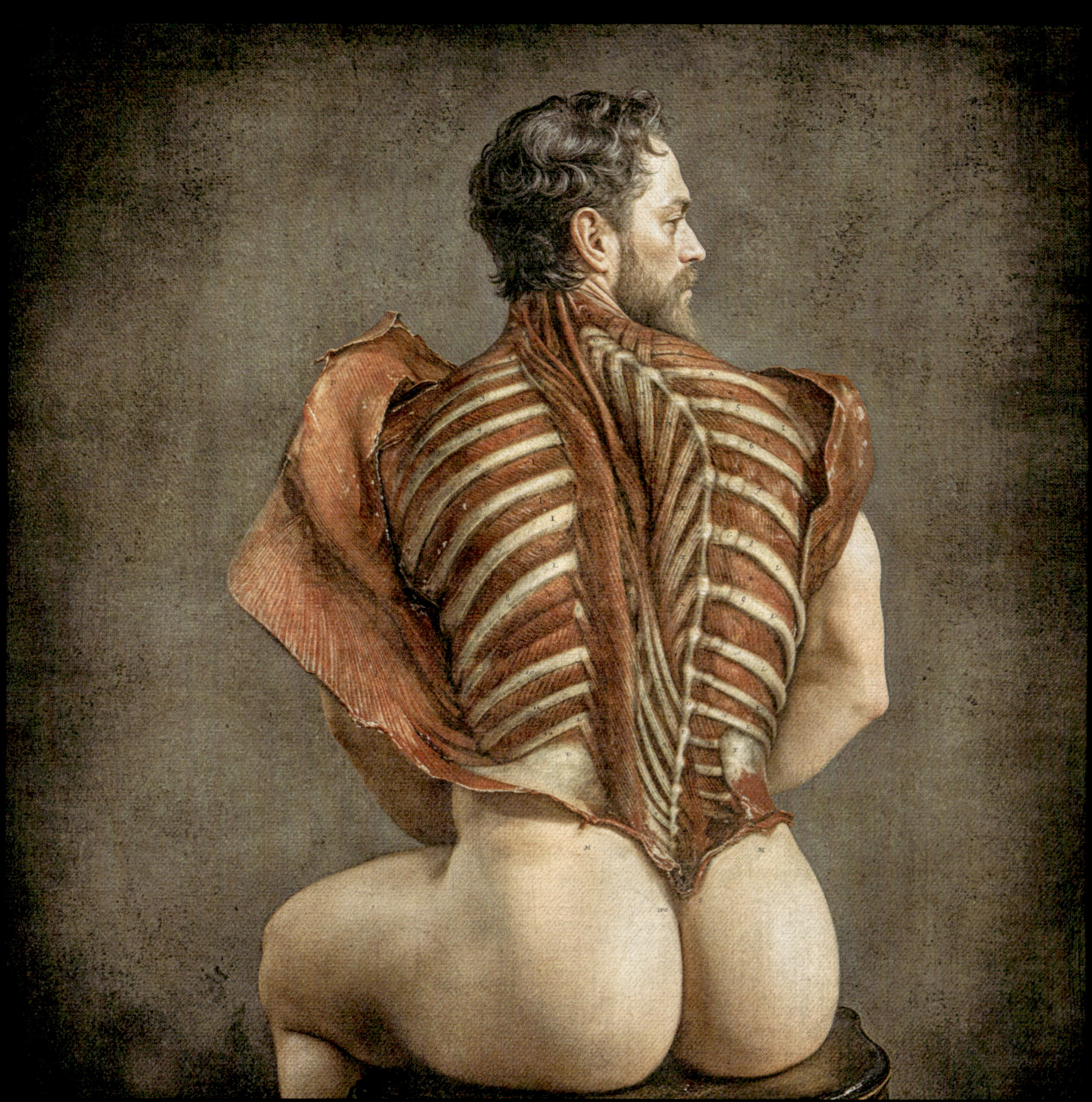

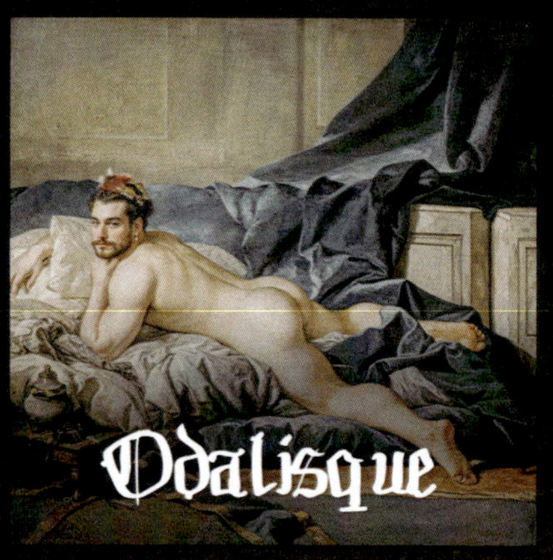

ASTRA ZERO REVAMP OF
THE BRUNETTE ODALISQUE
BY FRANCOIS BOUCHER, 1745

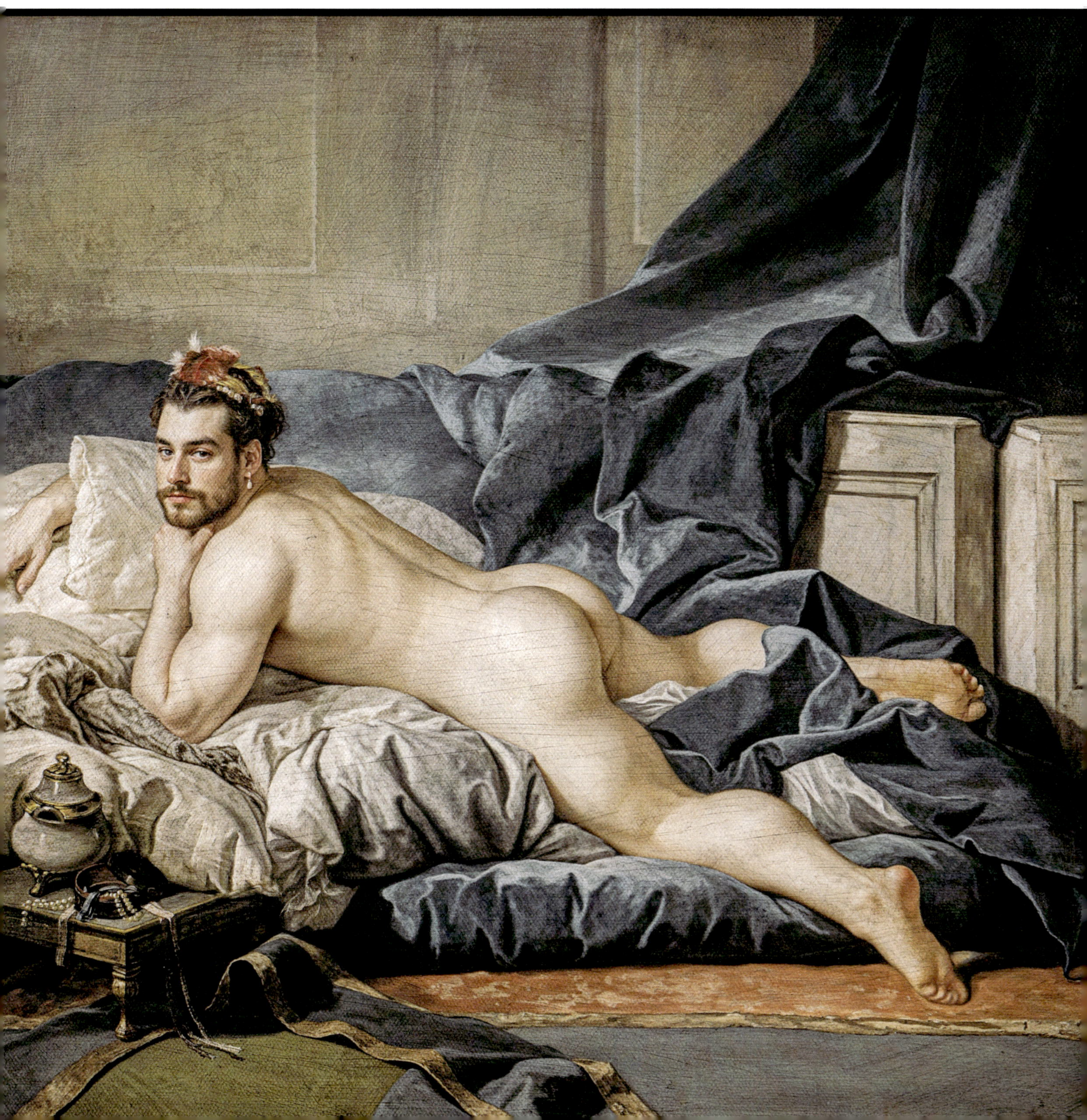

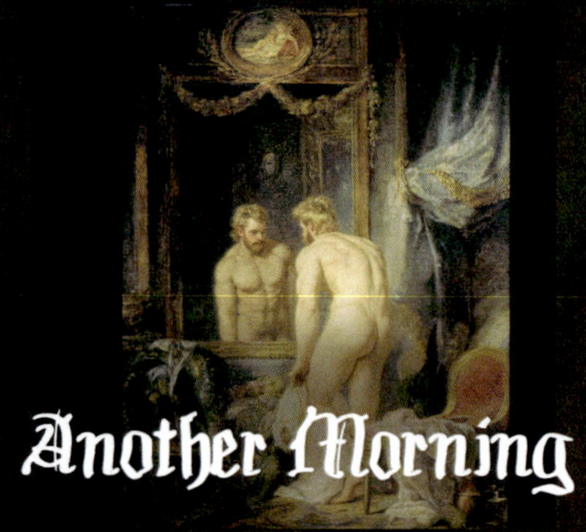

Another Morning

ASTRA ZERO REVAMP OF
MORGENTOILET, BY JEAN-FREDERIC
SCHALL, 1780-1820

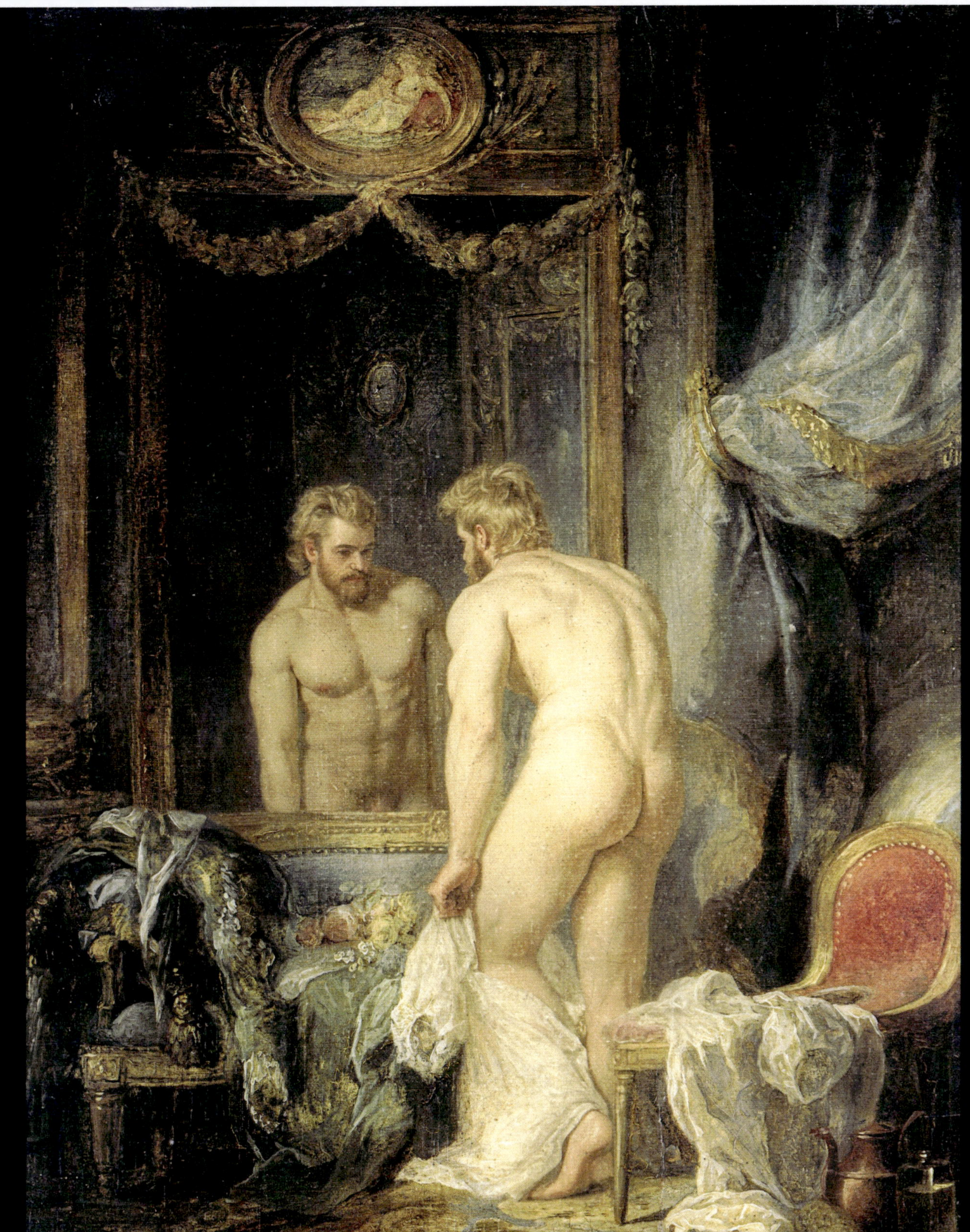

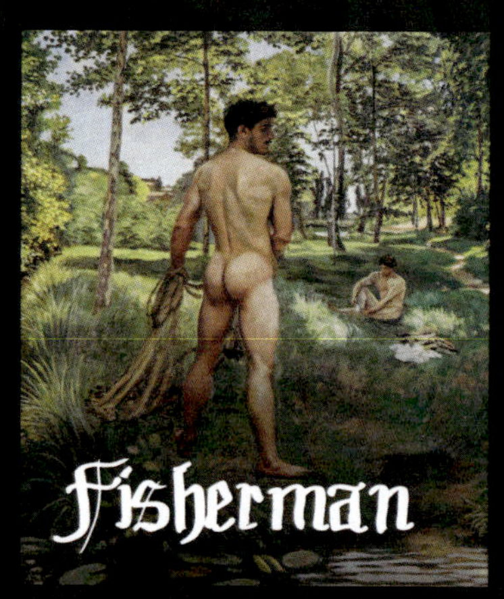

ASTRA ZERO REVAMP OF
PECHEUR A L'EPERVIER,
BY FREDERIC BAZILLE, 1868

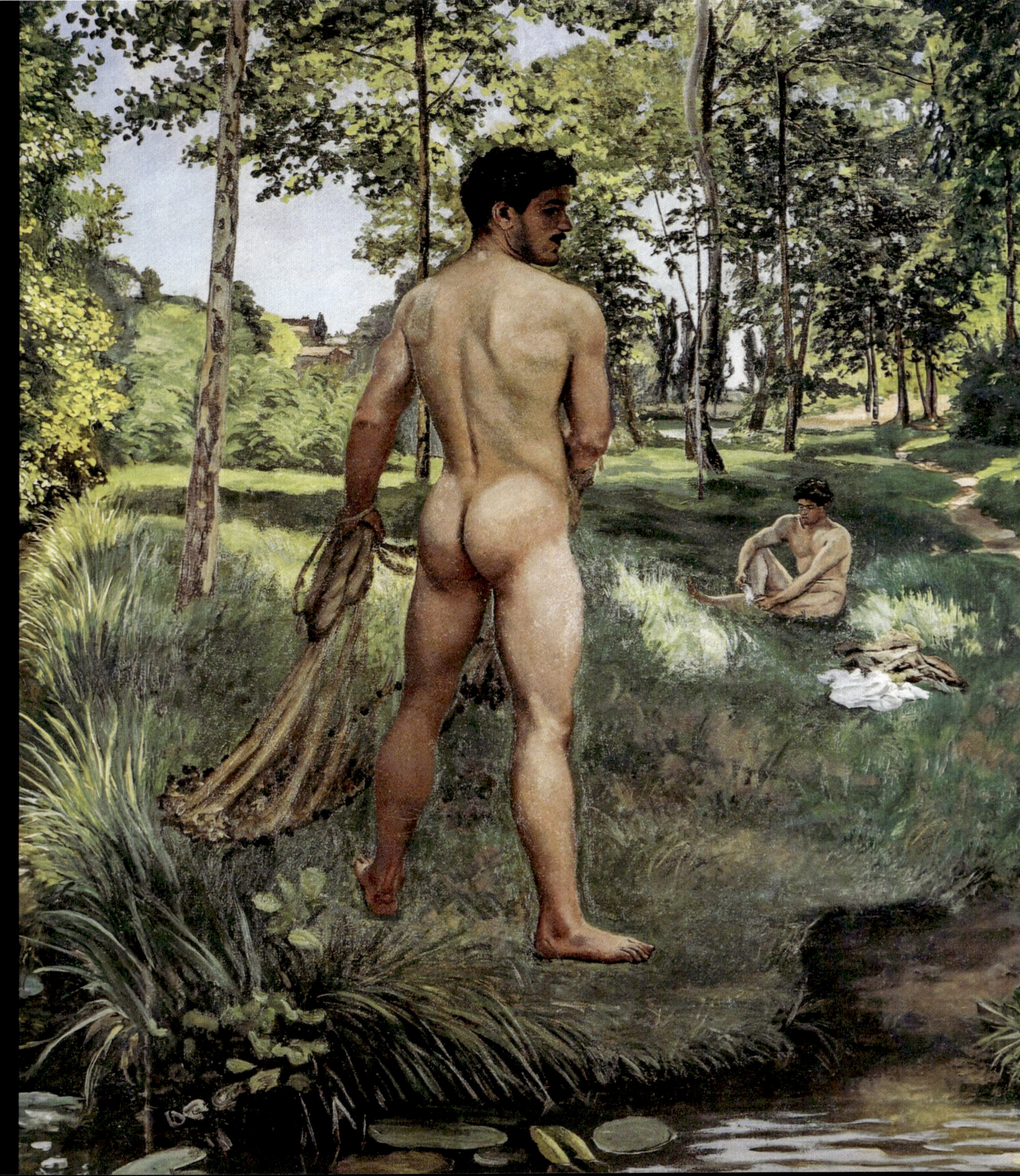

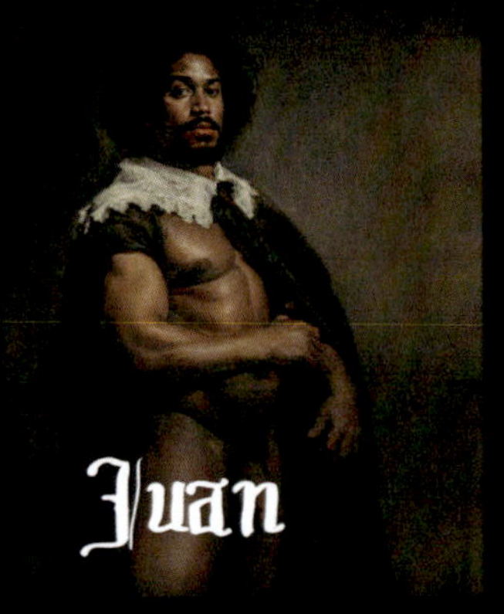

ASTRA ZERO REVAMP OF
JUAN DE PAREJA,
BY DIEGO VELAZQUEZ, 1650

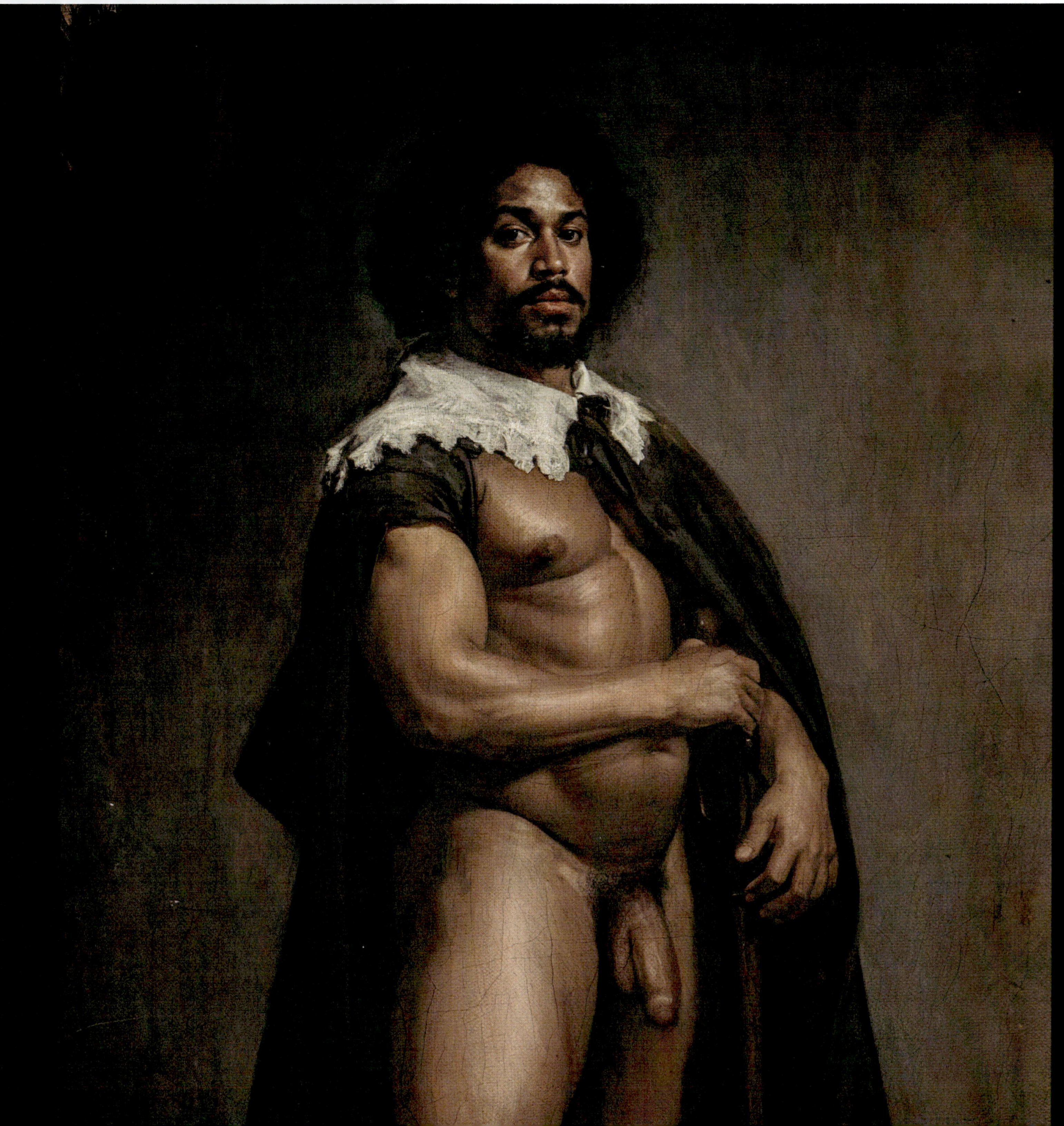

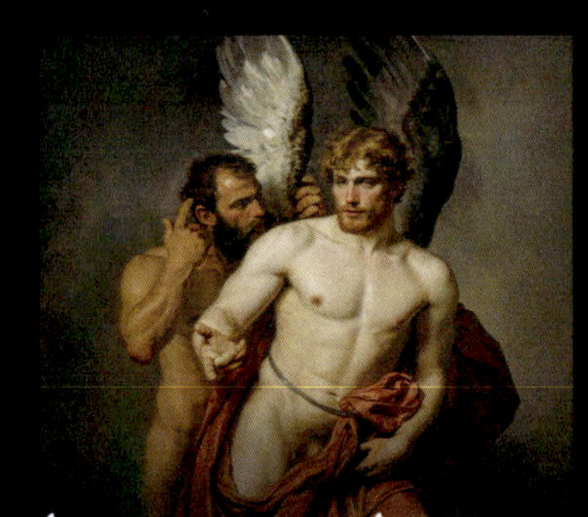

Daedalus and Icarus

ASTRA ZERO REVAMP OF,
DAEDALUS AND ICARUS, BY
ANTHONY VAN DYCK, 1615 - 1625

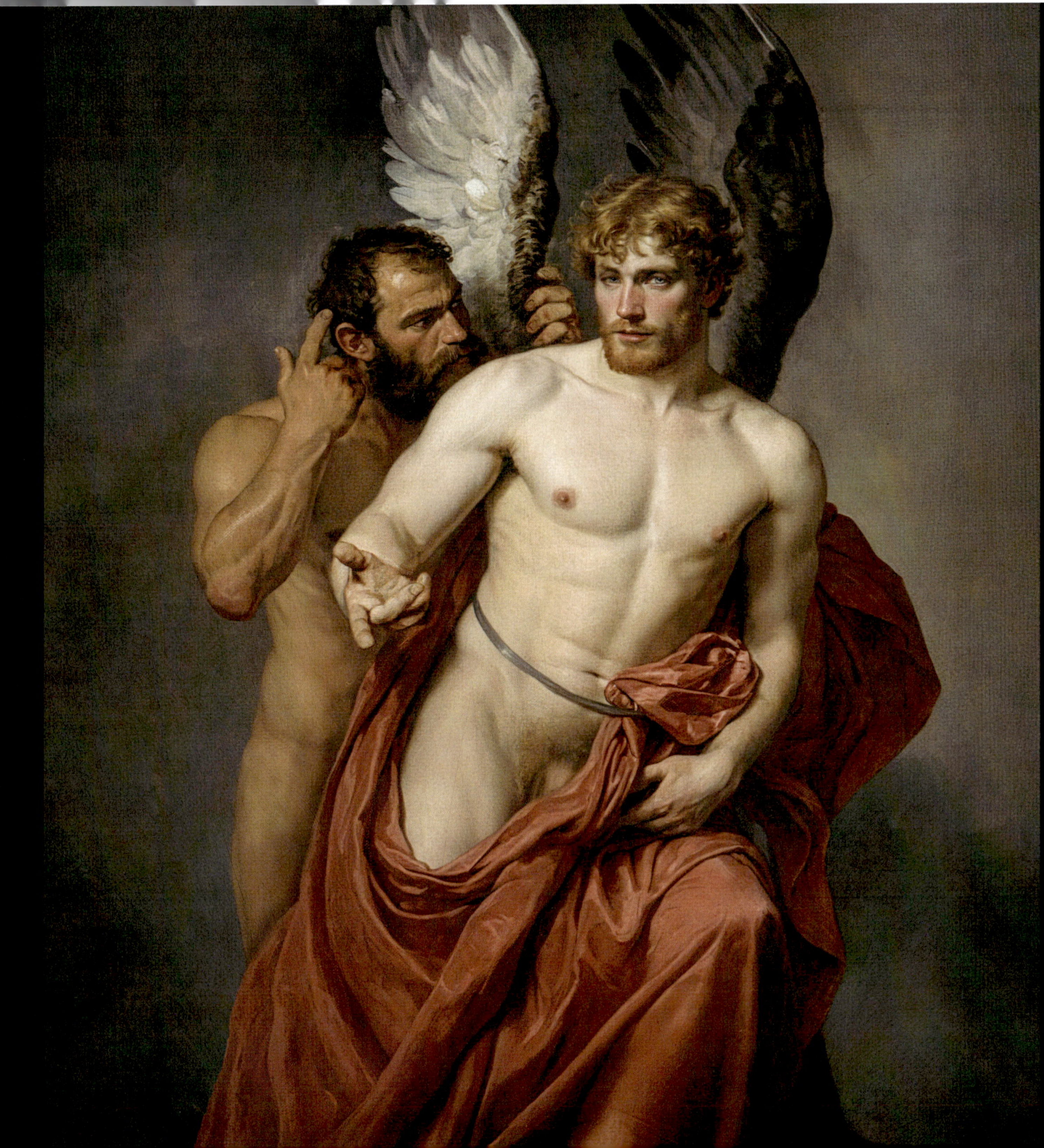

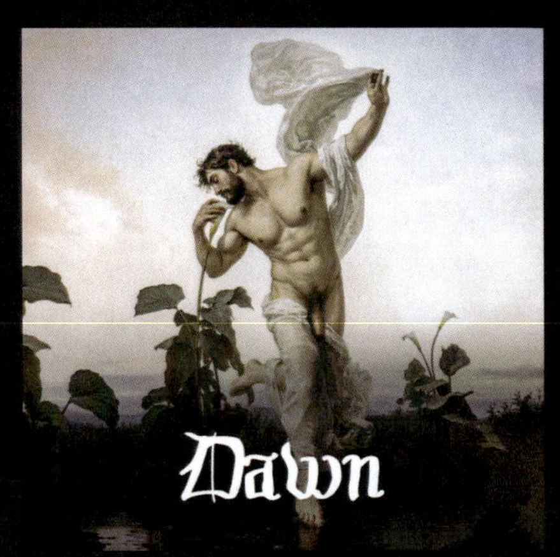

ASTRA ZERO REVAMP OF,
L'AURORE, BY WILLIAM-ADOLPHE
BOUGUEREAU, 1881

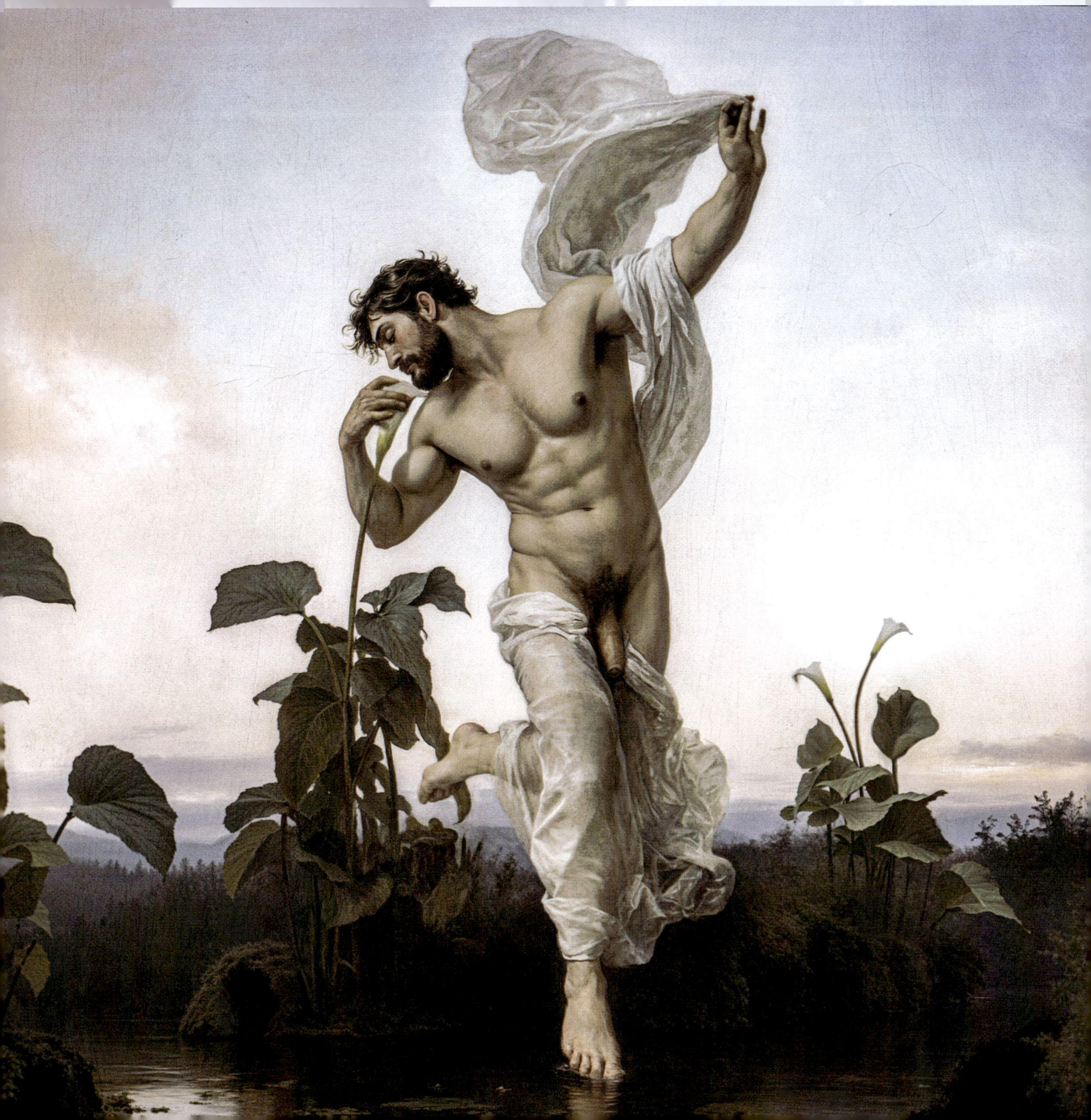

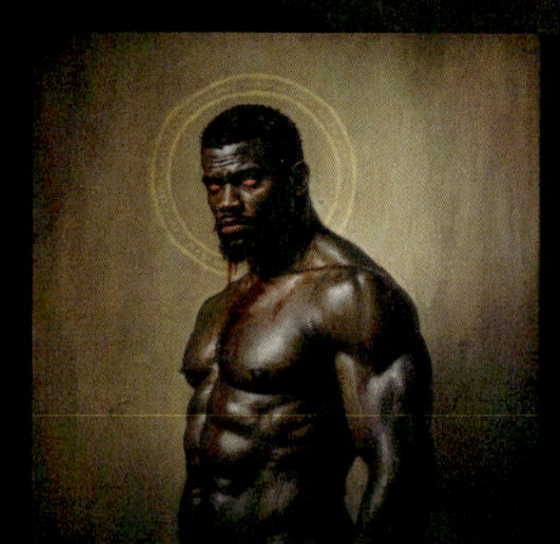

The first Immortals Son

ASTRA ZERO ARTWORK INSPIRED BY
VARIOUS PAINTINGS
FROM 1800-1900

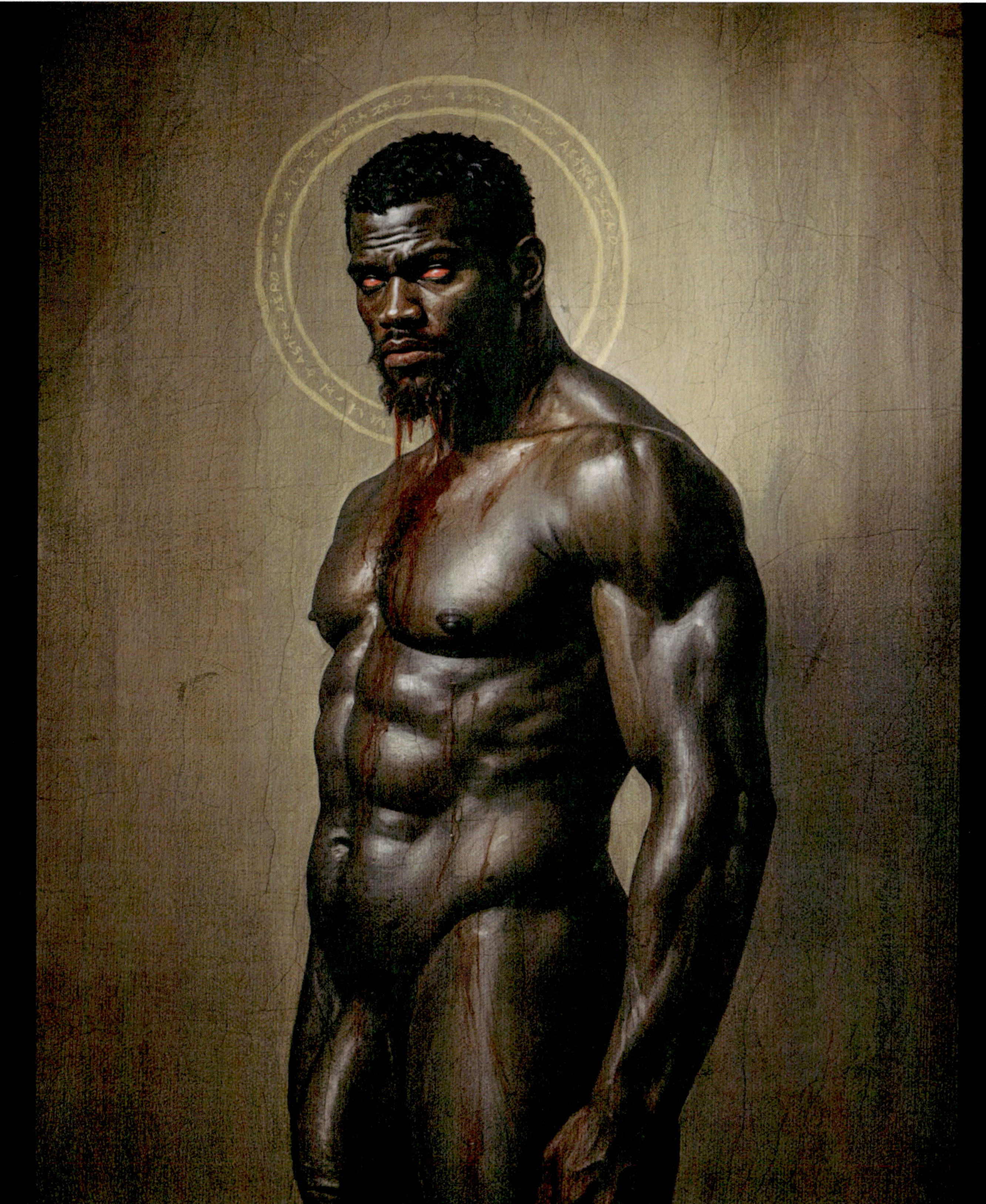

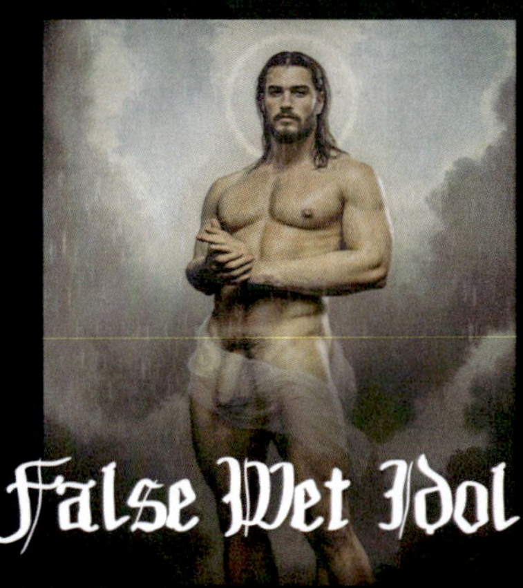

ASTRA ZERO REVAMP INSPIRED BY
VARIOUS PAINTINGS
FROM 1600-1800

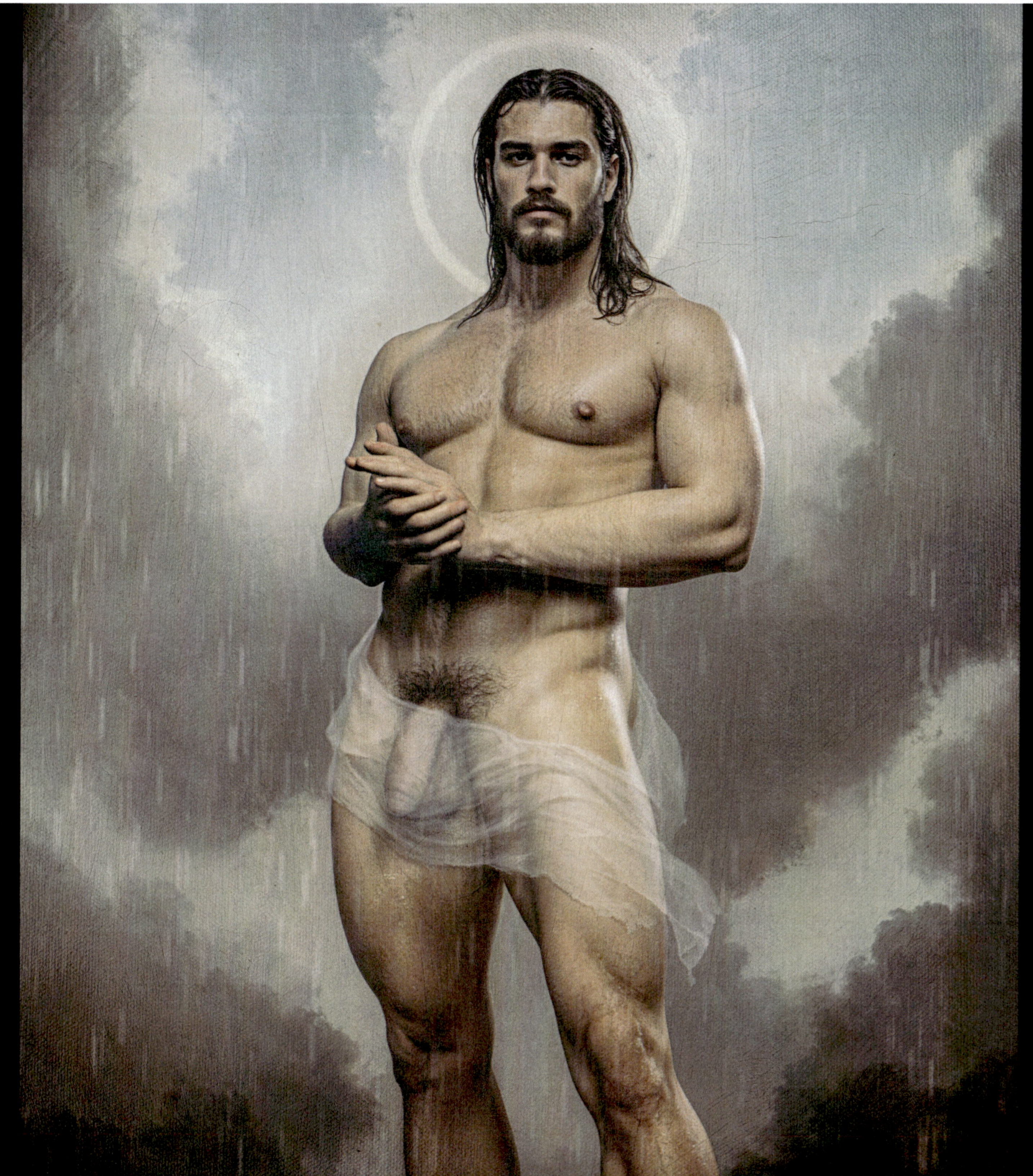

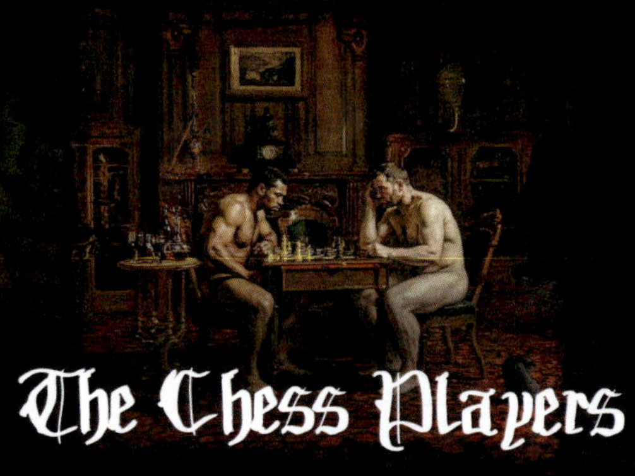

The Chess Players

ASTRA ZERO REVAMP OF
THE CHESS PLAYERS
BY THOMAS EAKINS, 1876

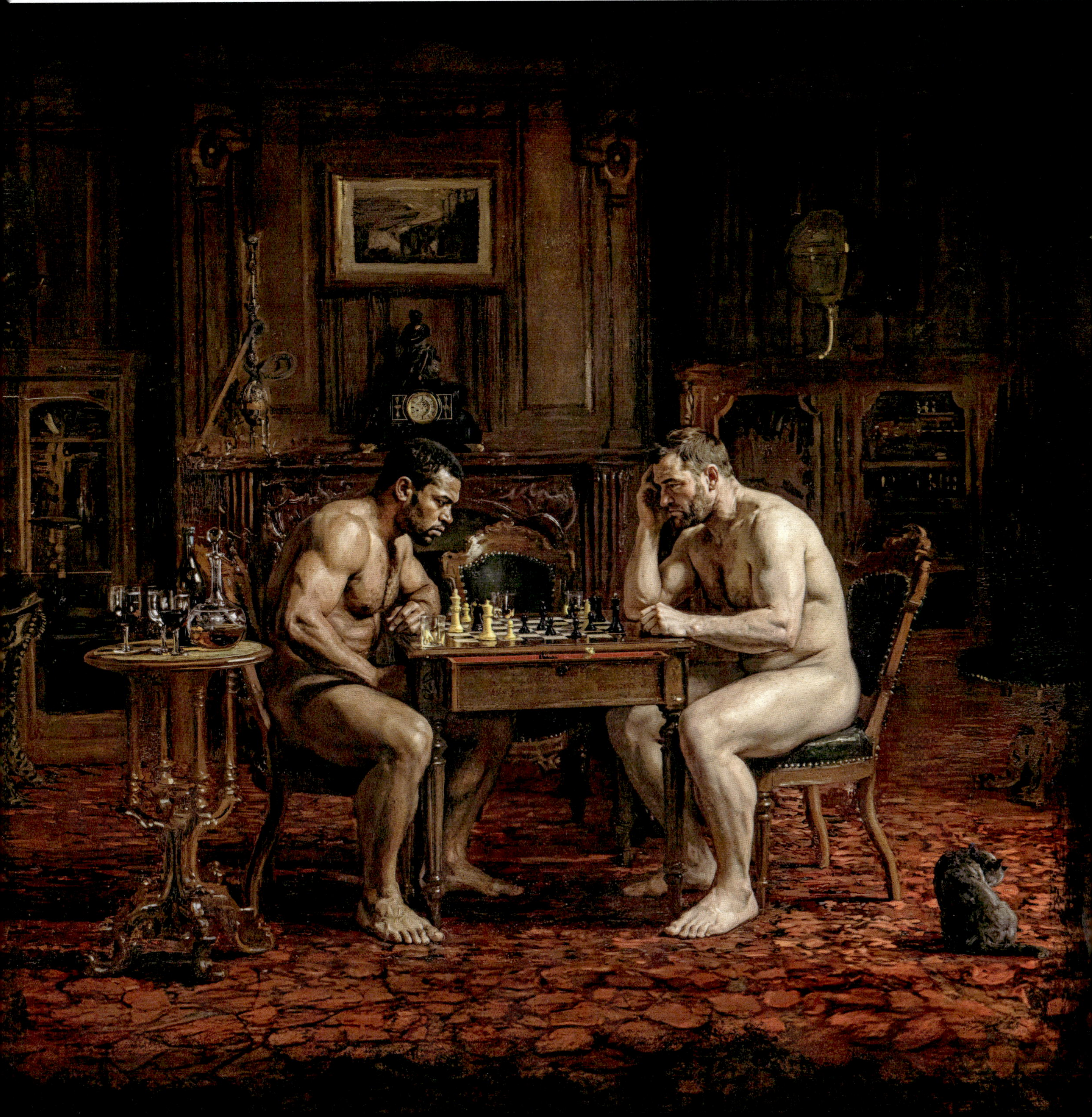

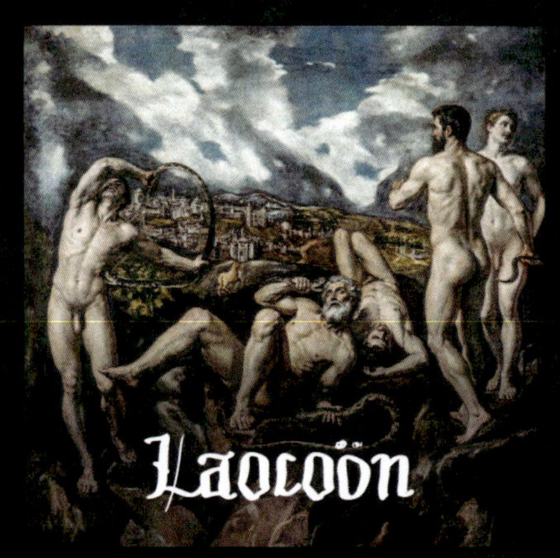

ASTRA ZERO REVAMP OF
LAOCOON BY EL GRECO , 1610

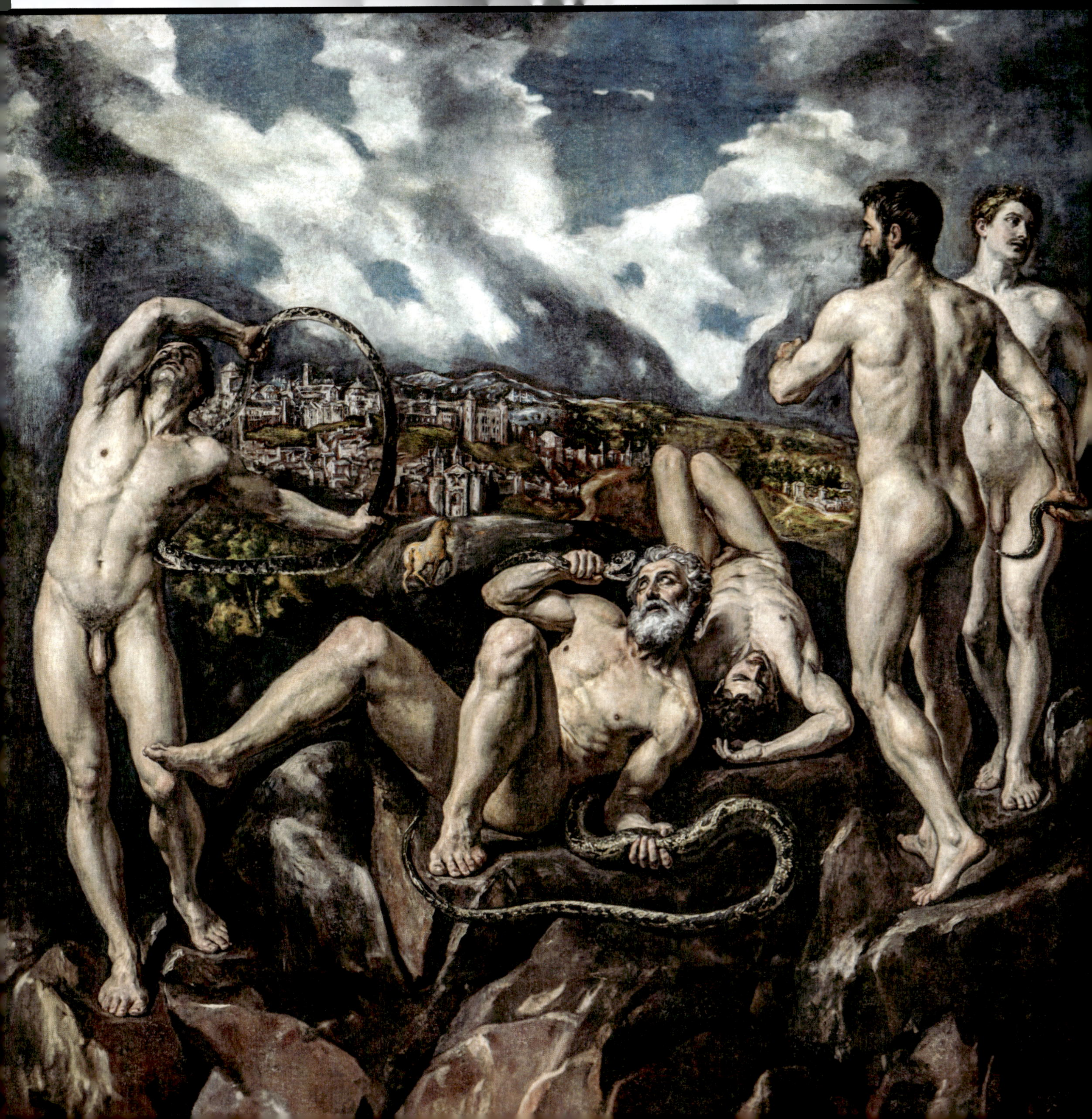

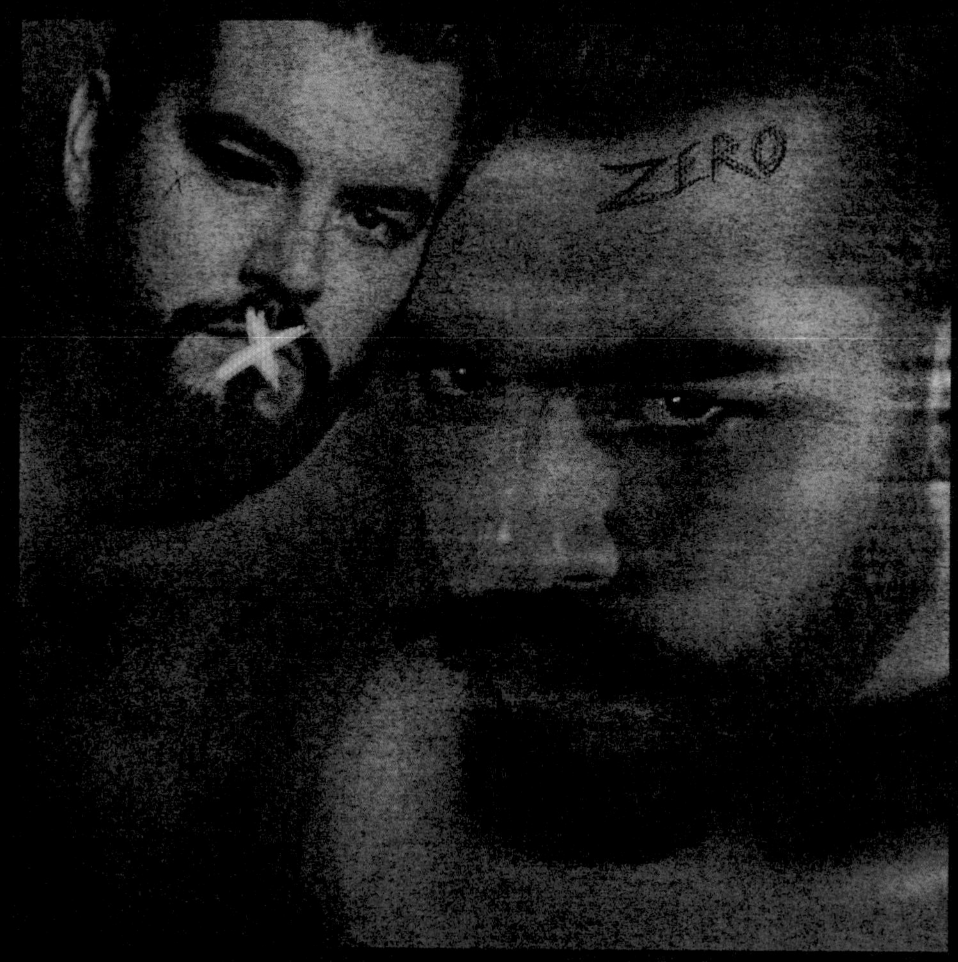

SELF PORTRAIT

About the Artist

Astra Zero (born Dustin Nicholls) is a queer Canadian alternative visual artist, designer, illustrator, video editor, creative director and songwriter.

His work fluctuates from a gothic macabre style and spooky cute themed visuals to his more popular sexually charged style of gay themed monsters, pop culture and historical revamped artwork with a dark erotic twist.

Starting off as a mainly 2D Artist with drawing & painting, His work has evolved to incorporate & mix more mediums and styles into his workflow, from Photography, 3D rendered work and digital painting, to animation, photo / video editing and graphic design.

You can see more of his work on social media @astrazero and on his website: www.astrazero.com